MW01594838

v

I Did It for Love

HERMION CHIDDICK

WestBow
PRESS

A DIVISION OF THOMAS NELSON

ISBN: 978-1-4497-2769-7 (e)
ISBN: 978-1-4497-2770-3 (sc)
Library of Congress Control Number: 2011917467

WestBow Press books may be ordered through booksellers or by contacting:

WestBow Press
A Division of Thomas Nelson
1663 Liberty Drive
Bloomington, IN 47403
www.westbowpress.com
1-(866) 928-1240

Printed in the United States of America
WestBow Press rev. date: 10/07/2011

This story is based on a true event, but all names and locations have been changed to ensure the privacy of the people. Please be advised that I was granted permission from my family to use their situations in my book, and they will be more than willing to furnish written consent if need be.

To Jesus Christ and all the broken women all over the world.

Acknowledgments

I WANT TO TAKE THE opportunity to thank Michelle Evans and her husband John for giving me a place to stay when I was homeless. Thank you so much for listening to the voice of God when He told you to take me in.

Claudette, thank you for all your financial help. I don't know where I would have been today if it were not for you.

I thank my friend Mike Lyons for his genuine support and encouragement through my walk with Christ. My daughter Tracy Chiddick for providing me with unconditional love.

My sisters Jacqulyne, Little Me, World, and my brothers Paul, Max, and Roger.

My nieces and nephew, Reds, Racquels, Samarah, Ding Ding, Daniel, King J, and all the others—I love you guys.

My dad for visiting me in jail and being there for me when I needed someone the most.

My high school professor, Mr. Daniels, who has impacted me a great deal. Your kindness and moral support have contributed a great deal to the woman I am today.

My church family at New Harvest for giving me a sense of belonging.

Pastor Davis, you are indeed a remarkable man of God. Thank you for teaching me the truth and bringing me closer to God.

I thank Mrs. Madge for being my mentor.

Mrs. Eunise, my spiritual mom and friend, thank you for being there at all times.

To Mrs. Renee for your pleasant smile and hospitality.

To Bro Anthony for emulating all the qualities I would love to have in a husband.

Mrs. Betty, Mrs. Minnie, Mrs. Fannie, Bro Eddie and Mrs. Rita for your constant encouragement.

To Trevor for being funny and cute. My roommate Nancy, you have really been a friend.

To Shernel Lewis for bringing out the best in me.

To my prayer partners and sisters in Christ, Komi and Nicole.

To Ashley Slade, thanks for having my back and being there for me.

To Fabbie and Kimon for helping me stay young.

Alicia Brown, my sis, my twin godsons. My goddaughter Ashley, my wonderful cousin Che Phillip. Wow, what can I say to the man who has taught me the importance of getting an education and encouraging me to go to Midwestern State University? Cousin, I would not have embarked on an educational path if was not for you. To Kassi, my beautiful cousin-in-law and friend in Christ.

To my husband, wherever and whoever you are, I want to thank you for praying for me in the same manner in which I am praying for you. Please know that I am saving myself. I pray that our love will survive the test of time, and we both will supplement each other in the manner that God intended.

Most importantly, I would like to thank Jesus Christ for believing in me. You have given me the tools to liberate myself from a life destined for destruction.

Chapter 1

MANY PEOPLE ASK ME WHY I ended up in jail and why I lived the life that I did in the past. What can I say? What reason can I honestly give? God has rescued me from a life characterized by sin and shame. The person I am today is a living testimony of the power of Jesus Christ in my life.

Growing up, I was exposed to all sorts of false religion. I really did not understand who God truly was until about two years ago. I now believe in Jesus Christ. He is the Son of God, and He is equal to God.

The Lord says, "He is not willing that any should perish, but that all should come to repentance" (2 Peter 3:9). My intention in writing this book is not to capitalize on wrongdoing, but to emphasize that—in spite of one's past—there is always hope for the future. Jeremiah 29:11 says, "'For I know the plans I have for you,' declares the Lord, 'plans to prosper you and not to harm you, plans to give you hope and a future'" (New International Version, 1984).

One of my greatest struggles in life was to come to terms with who I was an individual. I placed a high, unrealistic demand on myself. When I failed to live up to the unrealistic expectations, I resorted to men to provide a clearer meaning to my life—a life that includes walking completely outside of God's will.

Jail has taught me so much; during my restricted freedom, I was made free. I was free to decide what I really wanted to do with my life. I was tired of being unhappy and desperately wanted a way out. I was tired of using sex to measure my worth as a woman. I was almost ready to give up the notion that I needed to be with a man in order to feel good about myself. I was living my life to please others and not myself—afraid of what my friends would think about me being single.

For years, I dated men that I did not have many feelings for. I suffered a lot, hoping to one day find someone to fill the void that I felt deep down on the inside. I wanted love; I was willing to risk everything for someone to love me. The truth is that I always equated sex with love. As time went by, I developed a feeling of worthlessness and was plagued with the disease of loneliness. I became destructive to myself and others—that is why I believe without a shadow of doubt that my heavenly Father used the harsh reality of confinement to try to get me on track.

Looking back, I don't regret being incarcerated. During those shattered moments of my life, I decided to seek God's face. I spent a great deal of time reading the Bible and going to Sunday school. I wanted so much to embrace change, but it was hard.

Growing up, I was labeled as the bad kid—the one whose mother was an alcoholic. I was embarrassed of where I lived, the broken old wooden house with no electricity or inside toilet. All nine of us scrambled together like yard fowls. Deep inside, I knew there must be a better life. I wanted Jesus. I wanted to learn about Him, but I had no clue how to begin. The religion I was exposed to was contrary to the true religion of God based on the Bible. I did not know about the Holy Spirit. I knew Jesus died on the cross, but I thought He died for a group of people and I was convinced that I was not one of them.

My mom used to wear an eye necklace around her neck for protection. She said it was supposed to protect her from evil. Since I was a kid, I did not know any better. In my little mind, I knew that something was wrong. She used to go on mourning ground for days. Whenever I would ask her what it really meant, she said that it was her way of finding out things about the future. In my little mind, she was a hero. She would predict things that would happen just as she had predicted. She said she was born with a gift to discern things.

I am so happy that God delivered me from such darkness. The Holy Spirit took my hands and led me to the truth. My mom was hindering the call of God upon her life by seeking answers about her situation from evil sources. I am so happy that He sent His son Jesus Christ to die on the cross so I can be free.

I had no sense of direction growing up; I did basically what I wanted to do and lived my life the way I saw fit. I desperately wanted someone to love me—someone to hug or tell me how beautiful I was. My mom never kissed me or showed any affection toward me.

Sitting in jail opened my eyes to a lot of things. I had the time to reflect. I had to make a decision. I felt like someone was guiding me to make the right choice. It felt like someone was trying to say, "Hermie, there must be a better life—there is hope for you, and you don't have to live with such guilt and pain."

Part of my mind was assuring me that things could get better. The cells were very tiny. I spent most of my days sleeping and looking through the iron bars, imagining my escape. One day after my evaluation, I was told that I had to go on antipsychotic medications. Standing in line for my pills, I actually heard voices that were not there. My panic attacks increased and, after much-needed advice from my jail friends, I told the doctor that I wanted to discontinue my medications. My mental state improved days after I stopped taking my meds.

I followed the rules far and above my ability. Hoping that I would be released on the premise of good behavior, there were times when I hoarded peanut butter or cheese slices from my lunch. Nevertheless, I never considered it a serious offense.

In a dream one night, a man took my hands and carried me across the fields, I did not see his face. The next morning, I woke up and found myself crying, "Please, Jesus, save me. I don't want to live like this anymore. I want to change. This is not the life for me." I was crying profusely.

Later that day, a woman visited us, and she started teaching us about God and how He sent His son to die for our sins, and that we are all sinners. She was nicely dressed with long skirts and T-shirts. She was holding the Bible.

I lifted my hand and said, "You said we all are sinners?"

"Yes," she said. "We all have sinned and come short of the glory of God."

I started to think that maybe I didn't need to feel guilty after all. Maybe there was hope for me. Before I went to bed that night, I read the entire book of John. The more I read, the more I wanted to read. The Holy Spirit was revealing things to me, but I could not understand most of them. Nevertheless, I felt myself changing from the inside. I no longer had the desire to lie. I no longer felt hatred for the men who I thought had done me wrong. I was becoming a lot calmer. For the first time, I felt like there was hope.

I signed up for a computer class. When I graduated, I felt a great deal of accomplishment. Someone from the state gave some of us a test, and I scored very high in reading and language. The examiner was very impressed.

She said, "Ma'am, are you planning to go to school when you get out of here? You seem like a very smart person."

I looked at her with a big grin. Wow, someone thought I was smart. I ran to my room and told the other inmates what the examiner had said, and they were very happy for me. I really think my other inmates knew I did not belong in jail. During the first two weeks of being incarcerated, no one came to visit or put money on my commissary— no one wanted the responsibility of having to put up with me behind bars.

I spent a lot of time praying and crying out to God. *Please, Father, please let someone visit me. I am lonely.* I thought about how bitter my mother would have felt toward the person who betrayed me. My mom always taught me not to depend on anyone. I should have known better since I saw the way she was abused. At a very early age, she was introduced to prostitution by someone she trusted and loved. Every weekend, she was taken to the Banana Boat and was encouraged to sell her body for money.

Life's struggles have been my mom's education. Her tears were her source of strength—and her compassion was all she had to give. No one understood her; she was an alcoholic to most. Deep down, I always felt like life has been cruel to her. She worked so hard and never achieved anything. In all my life, nothing has distressed me much more than her death. I went to school, I worked, and I took care of my mom. There were so many things I wanted to do for her, but death robbed me of that opportunity. Whenever I was depressed about my mom, I would resort to sex. I guess it helped ease my frustration and guilt.

I was so caught up with the pleasures of the world that Jesus had no place in my life. It was only behind bars that I first experienced the love of Christ. I was slowing developing self-worth. I wanted to get to know God. I would repent for my sins on a daily basis and would think before I acted most of the time.

A few of the inmates formed groups to talk about Jesus Christ, and my heart grew fonder and fonder. One day, someone came to visit me and started putting money in my commissary account. I knew there and then that it was an act of God. When the person started putting money in my account, my faith began to increase.

A few of the inmates attended the church services. We were aware of the fact that our souls needed to be delivered. I knew that once I was set free, there was no way I was going to resort to my old life. I was going to get a job and provide for myself and my daughter. I started making the best out my life behind bars. I developed a positive approach and made a promise to God that I was going to start going to church and would serve Him for the rest of my life.

Since other people were less fortunate than I was, I would often share my groceries with my cellmates and anyone else that was in need. Bologna with bread and mustard was our daily meal; we were fed three times a day. They woke us up at four o'clock every morning for breakfast. Breakfast was not mandatory, but dinner was. I guess it was a preventative measure against someone intentionally starving to death.

Chapter 2

My life has been surrounded by shattered romances. I cannot remember falling deeply in love with anyone. In fact, I was afraid to give anyone a piece of myself. I saw all men as evil and was highly afraid of committing. I buried myself in the arms of men—those who gave me a false sense of security. They seemed to have provided me with much comfort.

There were times when I felt led by the Holy Spirit to meditate on 1 Corinthians 6:18. It says to flee fornication, every sin that a man doeth is outside the body but he who commits sexual immorality sins against his own body.

The Lord was very concerned about my life; He saw something in me that I could not see in myself. He wanted me to preserve my body as a living sacrifice to Him, and I thank Him every day for not leaving me in my old ways. Although His attempt to transform me did not occur overnight, I learned a lot from the experience.

During my childhood, I was ashamed of where I lived, and I was troubled at night by demonic activities. When God looked at me, He saw a beautiful woman who was searching for love in all the wrong places. He reached out His hands and embraced me at the lowest point in my life. I was hopeless.

He reminded me of John 3:16, which says, "For God so loved the world, He gave His only begotten son, that whoever believes in Him should not perish but have everlasting life."

I would never allow any religion to dictate how my relationship with Christ ought to be. Jesus taught me Himself.

I am most grateful that Christ has given me a clean conscience. I am not afraid to say that I was once sexually corrupt because I am totally free from the sin that had me bound. I no longer have nightmares. The Holy Spirit protects my sleep at nights. As a Christian, I never had a problem admitting my struggles. I knew deep down the promises that God made to me. In 1 John 1:9, He said that if we confess our sins, He is faithful and will forgive our sins and cleanse us from all wickedness.

I will never purposely pretend to project myself as what I am not. The only way one can truly accept you is if you accept yourself for who you are. Some people get offended when I talk about Jesus with much authority. They say, "Who are you to claim that you have such an intimate relationship with Christ?"

They don't have a clue where I have been in my life. Experiencing such healing power leaves no choice but living in victory. I had someone question my relationship with Christ; he claimed that I stated that I am married to Christ and that I kiss Jesus' lips in the morning and cuddle up in His arms at night. I was talking about it figuratively.

If someone is not as close to God as you are, it may raise concerns about how the Holy Spirit manifests Himself in your life. I am not trying to bash anyone, but I believe that, in order to totally serve Christ, one has to refrain from placing any limitations on His power. God can do all things—and if He chose to reveal Himself to someone in a manner in which He has never revealed to you, why doubt His capabilities.

I am not here to validate my relationship with Christ to anyone. I am just trying to use my life story to impact women around the world who have suffered a similar fate. I believe God is using me just as he used Abraham, Noah, Esther, and Rahab. He is certainly not a respecter of persons.

I am not a pastor; I have never even held a position in church. I was living in sin before Jesus rescued me. I wore tight, seductive clothing and my bust hung out. I never adhered to the concept of modesty, and I still sometimes struggle with the concept of dressing like a Christian. God is not looking for perfection, although we must strive to be like Him. He understands that we were born in sin; there are struggles that only Christ can deliver us from.

I would never intentionally judge someone based on their past. Christ did not judge me based on my past. In fact, He used my mistakes and enabled me to learn from them. Rahab was a prostitute, yet she was in the lineage of Jesus Christ. Paul once persecuted the Jews and Christ used him to spread the gospel of truth to all mankind.

If I recall clearly, Abraham once worshiped a false God. David, a man after God's own heart, murdered a man and took his wife. God is merciful and certainly does not view man the way in which men view each other. If that was the case, I would be left to die in my sinful ways.

As Christians, we need to spread the gospel of love—not hate. In my opinion, if a leader in the church falls, I think he or she should not be cast out of the church if he decides to repent. We need to lift up one another. In Ephesians 2:1 Paul said, "And you He made alive, who were dead in trespasses and sin." God has the power to restore lives.

Chapter 3

As a young believer, I was taught many things. One was to trust God with all your heart. Psalms 24:1 says "The earth is the Lord's and all its fullness, the world and those who dwell therein."

We cannot trust man because man does not own anything. Everything on earth belongs to God. I know it may be a hard concept to grasp for most, but there are a lot of consequences when we fail to give God credit for what He deserves. I went through a lot of disappointments because of my failure to truly trust in the Holy Spirit to guide me.

I never grew up in church; growing up, my mother performed a lot of rituals that were not of God. It took Christ to open my eyes to His truth. If God never blesses me again, I will still praise Him because He has delivered my soul from so much evil that I am fortunate that He has favored me.

My relationship with Christ is quite different from your relationship with Him. God meets us on different levels based on who we are and how we desire Him. He is not a respecter of persons; please don't interpret this the wrong way. For example, when I reach out to Christ, I was emotionally broken. My only quest at the time was to find love. I had to accept Christ as not just my savior, but as my lover and friend.

Whenever I felt alone, I would stretch my hand out and say, "Please, Father, in the name of Jesus, give me a hug." If I was depressed, I'd say, "Jesus, I want You to come and lie in bed with me. I need Your comfort." In my relationship with Christ, it worked perfectly for me.

Don't be offended when you read about my fondness and deep desire to be kissed by Christ or to be embraced by the Holy Spirit. The Lord taught me that if I exert all the energy and desire Him the way in which I once desired the world, I would definitely experience a love from Him that may seem unreal to others. Believe me—it is happening. I walk around with peace and joy in my heart—even when I am going through disappointments.

Those who can relate to this know that emotional instability is a terrible thing. It is the driving force toward destruction. I don't believe God wants us to be afraid of Him. Many religious leaders teach that, when you go in front of God, you have to use fancy Biblical words and dress a particular way; some believe that you have to have your head tied. God doesn't look at trivial things like that, He looks at our hearts and how sincere we are toward Him.

Ladies who struggle with promiscuity may feel obligated to have intimacy outside of marriage because sex defines your relationship. If this describes you, please refrain from devaluing your self-worth. Christ rescued us—not because of anything we did—because of who He is. Lift up your hands to God right now. Ask Christ to come into your heart and deliver you from emotional insecurity. Don't be afraid to love Him. Don't be afraid to talk of His power in your life when you start experiencing transformation.

Sometimes I would have long conversations with God, but I actually heard his voice once. I was driving home from school, and I was very hungry. A friend had given me twenty bucks to buy food, and I was eager to go to the supermarket. I was about to use the money to buy food, when a voice in my heart said, "Hermion, go home." I knew it was God.

When God speaks to you, He gives you an awareness that it is Him. I went straight home. When I walked into the house, my cousin had cooked the best meal in the world. It was one of my favorite foods: Macaroni pie with salad, chicken, and rice. I was elated.

I know God is real. I know Jesus is real. I know the Holy Spirit is real. There is only one God—three in one. They are not separate beings. I am certain that my heavenly Father is using my life to help others. Even if it means exposing some of my darkest moments, it is okay. I am doing it for Christ. It is the least I can do.

My life is not my life. It belongs to God, creator of heaven and earth. My life does not belong to Buddha, Mohammed, or anyone else. It belongs to Christ. He died on the cross to save me from my sins. Please, friends, we cannot be ashamed to stand firm in our beliefs. One cannot call themselves a Christian and make excuses for other religious beliefs that are contrary to our own. Remember there is only one way to God and that is through Christ.

When the Holy Spirit revealed to me that I was going to obtain a bachelor degree, I thought it was my mind playing games. I had quit junior college more than eleven years earlier. Returning to school was something I never imagined, but the Holy Spirit was right. I will be graduating with a master's degree. I can only say that God is powerful, and one can achieve anything with Him.

Chapter 4

As I think about my life's transformation, I realize how silly it would be for anyone to say that my experience with the Holy Spirit is not real. I don't think that anyone can truly understand God. There are things that God revealed to me that I still have trouble understanding, but I can explain what He has done for me.

Before God selected me, I lived in great fear and was consumed with loneliness. I was haunted at night by what I imagined to be evil spirits. I put my trust in things and was defiant to God. I never knew about the Holy Spirit until I was saved two years ago. My concept of God was that of a spiritual being that I could purchase whenever I needed His services. My motive toward God was never correct. I only prayed when I was in danger or needed a specific favor. I did not know that any individual could develop a bonding relationship with Christ.

My spiritual turning point from being an agnostic to a Christian began two years ago. The first thirty-two years of my life involved a series of disappointments. My life did not show any improvement until I was arrested. In jail, I decided to embark on a plan to improve myself. It was a tough call—giving up sex was the hardest thing I ever had to do. If you ask me how God did it, I really do not know. All I do know is that I am single. I don't have a boyfriend. I don't go on dates—or even try to meet men for friendship.

I believe that when the time is ready for me to venture out on that path, the Holy Spirit will let me know. I am no longer going to set myself up the way I did in the past. I have no problem waiting on God. I have no problem telling a man my morals about sex outside of marriage. Who would ever imagine that me—a woman who used sex as a drug—would one day promote abstinence? It was not my doing—it was only achievable through the power of the Holy Spirit. Please don't be afraid to dream big. There may be obstacles to face, but trust in the power of God and things will be okay.

Chapter 5

It is not fair for my readers to read about me without a clear understanding of who I am. Later in the book, you will read about my struggles with the flesh even as a Christian. I also snuck a man into my bedroom, but a strong conviction prevented me from ever committing another sexual sin.

The Lord has been very good to me—even when I was walking in disobedience. When He chastises me, the Holy Spirit brings to my awareness the main reason why I am being punished. It always brings a sense of peace. Please don't think that I am an authority on God's voice—I am not. I often have to pray on many occasions for God to teach me to hear His voice.

There were several instances when I thought the Holy Spirit was talking to me, but He was not. One day as I was driving out of my apartment complex, I saw a black object in the road. In the review mirror, I saw what appeared to be a bird stuck to the pavement. Its head was swaying back and forth. I felt as if I needed to go rescue the bird—I was almost certain that the Holy Spirit was asking me to.

A voice said, "Go rescue the bird."

I drove back to the object only to find out it was a piece of plastic bag stuck to the ground. I was flushed with anger. "Father," I said, "Why would you poke fun at me like that?"

I later realized that not every voice you hear is the voice of God. Another time, I was driving around with an empty gas tank. I felt as if

God was asking me to drive by the gas station to wait for a man in a green shirt to give me some gas. I drove by the gas station and waited almost an hour, but the man never came.

There was another time when I really thought that the Lord told me to go into the supermarket and wait outside for a lady who I was supposed to give a hundred bucks. I called my girlfriend and we were excited to see the work of God through us. I drove up with my last hundred dollars and stood outside the store, but no one came. I was so disappointed when I left.

God knows the hearts of all men; it is okay to make mistakes—as long as we learn from them. I know the changes that were brought about. My friends and relatives know the changes. I want my readers to know the changes that were brought about so you can experience true deliverance in any area in your life.

Living in Denial

When I was living in sin, I was living in a fantasy world. It was difficult to get a grip on reality. Although I knew that my lifestyle would lead me to a world of danger, I felt that I was completely lost, and there was no way I could get on track. I was mad at the world. I was filled with anger. I did not think that the Lord had what it took to peel away the deep layers of sinful desires that consumed me.

Over the years, I had listened to people talk about how God transformed their lives. A small part of me wanted to experience His power, but I was not walking in faith.

One experience really defined how the Holy Spirit was communicating with me. I was returning from the courthouse to my jail cell, when I heard song by Yolanda Adams. The chorus brought tears to my eyes.

So I'm crying out
Crying out to you
Lord I know that you're the only one
Who is able to pull me through?

I knew the Holy Spirit was leading me to repentance. I knew with great certainty that I had to get every negative thought out of my mind. Thoughts about men—their betrayals and empty promises—were consuming me. Depending on God meant that I had to totally surrender. No more playing games—no more lies and deceit. If I really wanted to experience the true hands of God, I had to figure out a way to trust in Him. I accepted Christ into my heart that same moment. The Holy Spirit used that song—those words—to draw me close to Him.

The woman who taught us Bible classes made references to Luke 8:54. When Jesus took a little girl by her hand and told her to rise, she became alive. In my mind, that little girl was me. I was slowly beginning to love God and myself.

In jail, I became very empathetic toward others. I believe that God was using what the enemy meant for bad to change into good. The biggest lesson I learned behind bars was not to allow your circumstances to get the better part of you. James 1:12 says, "Blessed is the man that endures temptation, for when he is tried, he shall receive the crown of life, which the Lord has promised to them that love Him." I reflected on that scripture a lot behind bars. I decided that I had to make the best out of life.

Chapter 6

THE EVENING I GOT ARRESTED was dreary. I had an unusual feeling that something awful was going to happen. I woke to the loud music of my neighbor. I jumped out of bed and ran into the shower. I was late for my beauty appointment. My phone rang just as I was about to get dressed. It was one of the many guys that I had dated. I told him to stay away from me and that it was really over. He accused me of stuff, and I was mad.

I jumped into my car and went to his place of employment. I was so upset that my mind was not clear. I proceeded to fight and picked up an object and threw it at him. It was all in anger. I was arrested, fingerprinted, and sent off to jail. The judge said that I did not need any anger management classes and that I was experiencing a lot of emotional problems. I told him that I had just lost my mom and sister and that I had a lot of anger. He was a very kind and understanding judge; he reduced my charges and told me to stay away from the victim. I spent two and a half months in jail.

Tormented by Spirits

Matthew 6:24 said, "No man can serve two masters; for either he will hate the one and love the other, or else he will hold to the one and despise the other. Ye cannot serve God and mammon."

Looking back, I believe that my mom had a false concept of who God really was. She was involved in occult practices. I believe that I was tormented because of the religion she embraced. It is not my intentions to scare anyone, but sharing these experiences shows the power of Christ over demonic activities. Once you are a Christian, the enemy has no authority over your life. I came a long way from being scared of the darkness—afraid to sleep alone at night. That curse was only broken when I decided to truly surrender to Christ and accept Him as Lord over my life.

It happened in the dead of the night, I was lying on the bed that my brothers and I shared with my mother. "Mammie! Mammie!" I screamed. "He is trying to get me! Please Mam help."

I managed to turn my head to the opposite side facing the window. There were cracks in the board. The trees were laughing at me. The wind was calling out my name. I was petrified. The Enemy was messing with my mind. I looked ahead, and a big ball of fire was heading toward me. "Mam! Mam!"

I was sweating and crying. I was screaming and begging for help until it finally dawned on me that my mom and brothers were fast asleep. My sister was sleeping on the floor close to the bed. My little heart was pounding. I wondered why no one was waking up.

The round ball of fire transformed into a long thin shape and flew into the ceiling. I looked at it in horror.

My mother said, "Hermie, are you okay?"

I could not respond. My entire body was paralyzed with fear. I remember drifting into a sleep and feeling a heavy force over me. I knew that—whatever the force was—I had been robbed of my innocence.

The next morning, I knew something was wrong. It felt as if someone had penetrated me, but there was no blood anywhere. I told my mom about my experience. She said I needed to pray before I went to bed and everything would be okay. "Gentle Jesus, meek and mild, look upon me this little child, pity me and pity my, suffer me to come to thee."

I prayed for weeks, but the torment continued. I remember going to school and getting in trouble because of my experiences at nights. No one ever cared enough to ask me why I was behaving that way; instead, I was labeled a bad kid.

Whenever the fowls climbed into the trees, I knew that danger was approaching. I would experience serious panic attacks. The darkness became my worst enemy. The cocks crowing were my only source of companionship; they signaled the approach of a new day. There were times when I would get out of bed and try to jump through the window. I have no recollection of that, but my mother suggested that I needed help.

Looking back, I wished my mom had turned to Jesus for help that day. I wished she had gone on her knees and prayed out loud in the name of Jesus. Instead, she dressed me in my favorite outfit and took me up to the country to visit a man who practiced witchcraft. His name was Papa; he has been dead over twenty years. He had a long white beard that was almost touching the floor. He lived in an old wooden house with his wife who was never allowed to utter a word. He greeted me nicely and handed me a candy. My mom went into the other room and whispered something to him.

He took me into the living room and began to pray. He told my mom that there were demons that were trying to kill me, and he would come to our house and scare them away. I waited patiently for Papa to come to our house. Every time I would ask my mother when Papa was coming to send the demons away, her response was always the same. "He is busy, Hermie. He is busy doing God's work."

I really did not understand what God's work entailed. I knew that Papa had powers and very soon he would protect me from demons. Three months after my visit, I was playing dollhouse with my friends and I saw a man walking toward our house. I recognized Papa's beard. My mom knew he was coming and everyone one went out to greet him.

"Hermie," my mom said. "Come inside. Papa is here."

I breathed a sigh of relief. I said good-bye to my friends and climbed up the stairs. Papa was talking to my mother for almost two hours before my mother got a bucket of water mixed with oil and bathed me with the mixture. Papa took a pen and wrote in Chinese on the partition. He assured my mother that the demons would never return.

Papa was right; after that bath, I was not affected by those evil spirits for a very long time. What Papa did was not of God. It was a ritual of the

Enemy. He used witchcraft to get rid of spirits. I was innocent and did not have clue as to what was really happening. Nevertheless, that ritual has had a negative impact on my life. I was led to embrace a false religion. When Jesus delivered me, every morning I wake up I had to plead the blood of Jesus over my life. I had to pray to break the generational curses that were on my family.

The Lord taught me how to fight spiritual warfare. He allowed the spirits to torment me only so He could use me to fight His battle. There were times when I felt as if the Holy Spirit was trying to assure me that the battle was not mine to fight. I am so happy that Jesus opened my eyes to the truth. He could have left me to continue walking in darkness, but because of His mercy, grace, and kindness, He delivered my soul from the pit of hell.

I learned that the devil works in subtle ways to keep people from growing in faith and from totally surrendering to God. It is very important to repent from our sins and constantly ask God for guidance and protection. As Christians, we need to ensure that we are not being influenced by demonic forces. We need to cover ourselves with the full armor of God.

Chapter 7

SOME PEOPLE MAY ASK WHY God allows certain things to happen to certain people. I believe God knows best. Isaiah 55:8–9 said, "For my thoughts are not your thoughts, neither are your ways my ways, For the heavens are higher than the earth, so are my ways higher than your ways, and my thoughts than your thoughts."

My two friends were being sexually molested. I remember one of them coming to me with blood in her underwear, and she made me promise not to tell anyone. Three months later, my friends went away. When my friends left, it broke my heart. I remember walking home that day and having my mother greet me with tears running down her face.

She said, "Hermie, they are gone. Thank God they are gone."

I am convinced that it was for the better, but it created a deep void in my heart and a great mistrust for men even at such an early age. I became a loner—and would spend hours in the bushes all by myself. I used to imagine that someone would adopt me and I would no longer have to live such an unhappy lifestyle.

As I grew older, I became fond of my mom. I started viewing her as someone who been through a lot of heartaches and pain. She told me that she started drinking alcohol at an early age and she would steal money from her dad to buy cigars. She never finished primary school; in fact, she got pregnant with her first child when she was only fifteen. Although my grandmother embraced the true doctrine of Jesus Christ, my mom did not share the same ideology.

Before my mom died, she told me that she had become a Christian, and she believed in Jesus Christ. She knew she was going to die. In fact, she told me that it was okay to let her go. She said that she was tired of living such an unfulfilling life, and she was ready to be with the Lord. During her stay in the hospital, many church leaders visited her and prayed with her. I am almost convinced that she accepted Christ before she died.

Sometimes we make choices in life that lead to destruction, but we must never forget that God is a loving and forgiving God and He is always willing to hear a broken and contrite heart. In spite of how far we stray, He always brings us back to Him. Even when I was out in the world, God always brought a sense of awareness about Him to my heart. However, like most of us who are not yet ready to listen to His voice, we often find ourselves rejecting Him.

When I look back at my life, I thank God. I believe with all my heart that God's power is infinite. He can certainly rescue us from whatever state we are in. At an early age, I decided to leave my mother's house and venture on my own. I was working as a primary school teacher making a decent salary of $1,167 a month. My mom did not mind that I moved away as long as I saved enough money to assist her with her bills—and I did.

I was so caught up in the world. I went to parties, drank, and got involved with the wrong crowd. I resisted every opportunity to go to church and was caught up with the desires of the world. There was a part of me that would sit and fantasize about becoming a Christian, going to church, and serving Jesus—but it just seemed somewhat impossible.

Chapter 8

IT IS MY SINCERE WISH that one day my family would turn to Christ. Psalm 14 says, "The fool has said in his heart, 'There is no God.'"

They are corrupt, they have done abominable works, and there is none that does well. I want my family to experience the power of Christ and His limitless love. I want them to strive for the stars and know that there is no power greater than the power of Christ. God sent His son to die on the cross to cleanse us from our sins. Only the blood of Christ can set our souls free. I remember reading Luke chapter 20:2, when the priest and scribes asked Jesus by what authority He was doing His work. What was going through my mind was the fact that we can only gain authority from God through Jesus Christ.

I believe that Christianity is the only true religion—and the only way to God is through His son. Psalm 1:1–2 says, "Blessed is the man that walks not in the counsel of the ungodly, nor stands in the path of sinners, nor sits in the seat of the scornful; but his delight is in the Lord and in the Lord he meditates day and night."

I believe as Christians we must never cast judgments. Romans Chapter 2 says, "Therefore you are in excusable, o man whoever you are who judge, for in whatever you judge another you condemn yourself; for you who judge practice the same thing."

We must live in love and harmony—and help those that are not strong in the faith. I am so grateful that the people God placed in my life did not ridicule or point fingers at me. I was embraced by my church and was offered a lot of spiritual support. I was assigned a mentor whose love for Christ and kindness impacted me a great deal. I thought that God loved us all and we all sin from time to time, but the most important thing was walking in victory—and not allowing sin to have dominion over our lives.

I am so grateful to God for taking me away from the hands of the enemy—from men who exploited and used me for their own gains. I was vulnerable and they took a great deal of advantage. They gave me money, but I was losing my soul.

The Bible says, "What does it profit a man to gain the whole world and lose his soul."

Jesus is incredible; I never thought that in my wildest dreams, I would one day become independent of men. I'd prefer to die than to resort to my old way of life. I never found fulfillment in the life that I was living. I was a very miserable person. Although I appeared to be happy on the outside, deep down I was miserable.

During the midst of my sinful ways, God was warning me. He was signaling to me to give up my old life, but I was in too deep. I did not think that God had enough power to rescue my soul. I would often tell Him to take a chill pill. "Can you pick up that pen on the table for me, Jesus? If you do, I would serve you forever."

I would tell myself that He was powerless and that I was justified in not serving a weak God. I always thought that evil was stronger than good, and evil people had better chances of attaining happiness than good ones. The good people I knew who worshiped Jesus were either poor or on a sickbed. There was no way I was going to subject myself to that kind of calamity. The Bible taught me that life is about making choices. It teaches us to abstain from evil deeds and—with everything—trust in the Lord.

Chapter 9

BEFORE I BECAME A CHRISTIAN, I blamed a lot of my downfalls on my upbringing. The Holy Spirit taught me that acceptance and forgiveness are crucial toward the healing process. I hated men and, although I was dependent on them for sex, money, and emotional support, deep down I knew that their intentions were not genuine.

I never got a spanking growing up; in fact, I was pampered and treated much better than my brothers and sisters were. I really do not understand where all that hatred came from. I know I was born for a purpose. I believe that God has given me so many chances. When I was born, I weighed two pounds, eleven ounces. The doctor said that I was not going to make it. So my mom stole me from the hospital. I guess God kept me alive to one day do His will.

I had a terrible upbringing and an unstable home. I was in desperate need to find love in all the wrong places. I never got a hug from my parents. I never heard I love you. Yes, they provided for my basic needs, but my self-esteem was shattered. I had no value placed on my life. I was very impulsive and made all my decisions in haste.

When I was about twenty-six, I went off and married a man I hardly knew. Two months before giving birth to what would have been a beautiful baby, I was kicked out of my home. I remember walking into the abortion clinic with a friend waiting for me in the parking lot. I remembered one of the nurses begging me in secret to have the baby and maybe consider adoption. I could not—she did not understand that I had no place to live.

Chapter 10

GOD HAD TO INTERVENE; I was really destroying my life. I had no morals. I was battling feelings of anxiety that stemmed from emptiness. In spite all my relationships, nothing provided fulfillment. My life was guided by the expectations of others. I was a people pleaser; it was very hard for me to say no. I needed friends to love me; I would give away my last dollar as long as it would secure somebody's heart.

Deep in my heart, I knew I had potential. People would tell me all the time that I was very smart, but even if I knew that I was, I avoided success so I could make friends. Most of my friends had no bright prospects for the future. In order to feel accepted, I had to become just like them. I felt the hands of God even during my darkest moments. God was there for me when my mother died. He was the one who was there for me when I was being followed by a madman in the bushes who had a machete in his hand to kill me. God was there when I was homeless on the streets of New York and had nowhere to turn. God was there for me when my sister died. God prevented me from being raped by a total stranger.

God had my back; He saw something in me that I could not have seen in myself. There was a small part of me that assured me that I was beautiful—and that small part of me was the Holy Spirit trying His best to deter me from living a life with such regret and shame. In spite of God's effort, I lived my life in pursuit of love even—if it means going against the very reason why He sent His son to die on the cross.

Waiting for Mr. Right

I know that when Mr. Right comes along, I will be able to give him a part of me that will satisfy him completely in so many ways. I know that there is a Mr. Right somewhere for me. I just have to continue to keep my body pure. I am not allowed to go on a date—or even have male friends over at my place. I have tried doing that before and felt miserable.

I believe the Holy Spirit is guiding me to refrain from all tempting situations. One of the things that I have learned during my walk with Christ is that we feel a lot desires, but we cannot always live to satisfy them. We cannot live a double life. Once a person experiences the true healing power of Christ in their lives, it is very hard for them to turn back.

When Christ took me out of my darkness, He exposed me to a type of life that I did not know existed. He gave me a sense of security that I had never gotten from the world. I used to worry a lot about situations, but now I have a sense of peace about almost everything. I learned to walk in the spirit and not look at life from the world's perspective. From a man's perspective, there is no solution for the world's biggest problems. People are frustrated by hurricanes, famine, and other natural disasters. But from the perspective of someone that is walking in the spirit, we learn to embrace catastrophes with a smile. I believe that God has the power to do anything. His power is not limited. I know where God took me from. He has established my feet upon a rock, and I am happy to encourage others who are lost to turn to Christ.

Concerns and answers that will help strengthen a person's walk with Christ:

Q: I find it very difficult to turn from my evil ways?
A: The Bible says I can do all things in Christ who strengthened me. "When we decide to give up our sinful ways, it is not us who are doing so, but the Holy Spirit who is guiding us" (Philippians 4:13).

Q: God cannot save me—my sins are too many.
A: The Lord is not man; His power is infinite. "The Lord said, Come now, and let us reason together. Though your sins be as scarlet they shall be as white as snow, though they be red like crimson, they shall be as wool" (Isaiah 1:18).

Q: I believe in spirits other than the Holy Spirit.
A: The Lord said, "Regard not them that have familiar spirits, neither seek after wizards, to be defiled by them: I am the Lord your God" (Leviticus 19:31).

Q: My boyfriend is a pastor. He loves the Lord. Is it okay for us to be intimate?
A: No! Fornication is a sin—it does not matter who you are committing it with. You should refrain from all sinful desires. If a man is truly of God and is guided by the Holy Spirit, he would not subject himself and you to that sort of behavior. Proverbs 6: 32 says, "Whoever commits adultery with a woman lacks understanding: he does it destroys his own soul."

Q: I am afraid of losing my boyfriend.
A: One of our biggest problems is the desire to be loved. We are not primarily concerned about having sex. We just want affection. Sometimes because of our strong pursuit to be loved, we find ourselves in compromising situations. When it comes to feeling important, we need to have someone to love us. Well, it is okay to have those desires, but we cannot jeopardize our relationship with God to please a man. God must come first in every aspect of our lives. We find ourselves yielding to tempting situations because we are afraid to say no, we are afraid to lose favor with a man. When we are faced with such a situation, cry out to God and ask Him to give you the strength to put Him first in your life.

Q: I cannot stand church people. What can I do?

A: "Therefore thou art inexcusable, O man, whosoever thou art that judgest: for wherein thou judgest another, thou condemnest thyself: for thou that judgest doest the same things. But we are sure that the judgment of God is according to truth against them which commit such things. And thinkest thou this, O man, that judgest them which do such things, and doest the same, that thou shalt escape the judgment of God? Or despises thou the riches of his goodness and forbearance and longsuffering; not knowing that the goodness of God leadeth thee to repentance? But after thy hardness and impenitent heart treasurest up unto thyself wrath against the day of wrath and revelation of the righteous judgment of God" (Romans 21–5).

Chapter 11

The Lord said, "What iniquity have your fathers found in me, they have gone far from me, and have walked after vanity, and are become vain? For my people have committed two evils, they have forsaken me the fountain of living waters, and hewed them out cisterns, broken cisterns that can hold no water. Thine own wickedness shall correct thee, and thy backslidings shall reprove thee: know therefore and see that it is an evil thing and bitter, that thou hast forsaken the Lord thy God, and that my fear is not in thee, saith the Lord of host" (Jeremiah 2:5, 13, 19).

Those were the Scriptures that the Lord had me meditate upon when I walked away from His word. I had started going to church with one of the ladies I met in jail. I went to church out of obligation for two months.

Mrs. Joy got me a great job. She wanted me to get on my feet. In less than two weeks, I got fired because I was flirting and exchanging rude messages with one of the employees. Yet Mrs. Joy was very supportive. In two months, I quit going to church. I could not understand the sermons, and I had no interest in the things of God anymore. Whenever I did go, I would be looking at my watch, praying for the service to be over.

I forgot all my promises I made to God while I was behind bars and slowly resorted to my old ways. I started dating men on the Internet just to go out to fancy restaurants and toss them aside. It was something to do for fun. I was heartbroken and disappointed in a relationship when I decided to really to surrender to God for the second time.

I met a handsome guy that was different from all the men I knew. I wanted to date him. He never pressured me for sex; even when I offered, he said he wanted to get to know me first. He took me to fancy restaurants and said he really liked me. One day while we were out to dinner, I told him that I really liked him and I believed we could give it an honest try. He promised to take me out the next day. I agreed.

When he did not call the next day, I was devastated. I could not understand why he would mislead me like that. I went into my phone and erased his number so I would not have any way to call him. That hurt me a lot because I was planning to dedicate my heart to this man. He rejected me. I cried out to God like never before. "Jesus! Jesus! My heart is empty, if you can take away my pain, I will serve you forever." Instantly my pain disappeared.

I started reading my Bible. I felt a big relief. That day, I took pride in calling my old boyfriends to warn them that I was now a real Christian. I was no longer interested in playing games. I wanted Christ in my heart and I was not prepared to let anything stand in my way. God was fighting numerous battles for me.

I saw my physical and spiritual life transforming. I was going to church regularly. I started going to the Faith Center Ministries where I met a lot of lovely folks who impacted me tremendously. I spent three hours every day with God and fasted three times a week. All the anger and resentment I felt toward people who had hurt me in the past had subsided. I was hungry for the word.

I started taking Bible classes at a university and excelled. I believe the Holy Spirit was passing my exams for me. I was an all A student. It was a time in my life when I never thought of compromising my relationship with God. He communicated with me in ways that often blow people's mind. I knew very early in my Christian walk that as long as God existed, I was destined for great things. My spiritual life was very good. I had lots of support from friends and people that I met in church. When they heard what God was doing in my life, they were very excited for me.

God opened numerous doors for me. He even granted me favors from people that did not like me much. I was convinced of my victory in

Christ, but I was barely prepared for what would be considered some of the most serious sexual struggles in a Christian woman's life.

For a year, I was able to resist fornication. I came close to giving in on two occasions. One day I visited an ex-boyfriend of mine. We were on the bed—and I felt as if the Holy Spirit was instructing me that I should go. I said, "Father, you don't trust me. I have this under control."

As the guy started kissing me, I was becoming weak spiritually. I imagined someone appearing in the room and saying, "Hermie, what are you doing?"

I believe that the Holy Spirit was trying to prevent me from making a mistake. I stood up asked him to leave because I should not be alone with him. God would be mad with me. The guy was somewhat afraid; I pushed him out of the bed and locked the door. I cried and cried for almost two hours and begged for forgiveness. "Jesus," I said, "if you forgive me, please wake me up at midnight to worship you."

At midnight, the Lord woke me up.

"Thank you, Lord. Thank you for forgiving me."

I know this scenario may seem strange to most, but it is the truth. He was determined to keep my body holy. I remember entering what I considered to be a covenant relationship with God, assuring Him that I would never fornicate again. Little did I know that God was preparing me to have myself tested to prove to Him whether or not I was committed to keeping my promise.

Chapter 12

I WAS CRYING PROFUSELY IN my bed with my head buried in my hands. I looked around at the room and my entire life flashed in front of me. There were piles of garbage and dirty clothes. I had promised God that I would try my best to keep my room clean, but I was going through a depressing moment and cleaning was the last thing on my mind.

I wanted to hide from the outside world. It was the summer of 2009. I knew it was God's idea that I moved out of my area. He told me that I really needed a change.

I had said, "Father, if it is your desire for me to go to away, please let me know."

I was led by the Holy Spirit to open a book. The book said, "It would be good if you go away."

I knew that it was God's response to my question. Things at home were not working out exactly the way I would have liked them to. I had just accepted God in my heart, and I had to make a lot of significant changes. After being kicked out of my home, I was homeless. I went to live with a friend who I had no intentions of being intimate with—I did not want to compromise my dignity as a Christian. I packed my clothes in my car and left. Later that evening, I went to church and a woman walked up to me and said that God told her to take me in to live with her and her husband.

In my hometown, I made a vow with God to never, ever sleep with a man again. I went a few months without breaking that vow, and I was convinced that fornications were things of my past. He took me from my comfort zone where I had a big support system and brought me to a little city where I knew no one.

When I moved into my apartment complex, I noticed that it consisted of mainly young men and women—educated people who had left their homelands to pursue higher degrees. No one had prepared me for this; no one told me that after God groomed you, He usually tests you. Had I known that, maybe I would not have betrayed Him the way I did. It certainly did not take me long to get caught up with the lifestyle.

I met a guy that I was attracted to—he was not a Christian—and we started dating. I allowed myself to forget temporarily all the promises God had made to me and the plans He laid before my eyes. I temporarily allowed myself to forget how He rescued me from jail and gave me plan to better myself. I temporarily allowed myself to forget how he prevented me from diseases and kept food in my mouth and clothes on my back. The Lord had granted me favor with the judicial system and with school. I had graduated with honors—just as God had promised.

I knew I had to take immediate action. My life was falling apart; I was regressing into my old habits, and it was scary. As much as I wanted Christ, I also wanted to experience the satisfaction of pleasing myself. Eleven months of walking in sobriety came to a painful halt. My past struggles that I thought I had overcome presented themselves again. "Father!" I screamed, "I wanted so much to please you."

At that moment, I began to lose hope. I could still hear the voice of God, soft and gentle, assuring me that all was not lost. I could still feel His warmth. His tender touch insisted that I would be okay, but my mind was slowly condemning me. "How can a woman who is earnestly trying to seek God lack such discretion? You are no good—God will never be pleased with you."

It was the voice of the enemy trying his best to deceive me. Yes, I was very ashamed of my actions, but deep down I wanted to get up and live right. I remember my promises to God; I would never get close to a man again. I often wondered what God was thinking knowing that when I made those promises that I did not mean them. And even if He knew that I was going to regress, He still protected me and never removed His favor upon my life.

"Father! If you forgive me just this one time, I promise that I will never ever hurt you like this again."

I got up and walked around the room. I wanted to show God how serious I was at this point. Although I had repented earlier, I wanted to express myself through a song. I picked up a Ceci Wynas CD and put it into the player.

I said, "Father, I am dedicating this song to you. Please, Father, imagine that You are hearing this song for the first time in your life. Please, Father, imagine that you are sitting on your throne and Jesus told You that I have a song to dedicate to You and You are all excited waiting to hear it."

I grabbed a deodorant bottle and started to sing. I enjoy role-playing with Christ. I enjoy imagining things. I danced, sang, and put on a concert for Him. I picked up the bottle and started to sing. "I tried to reach out for you, but I fell. Time seems so close yet so far. All I need is another chance. I need to know Your mercy. Please, Father, forgive me. I want to do right by You this time."

I remembered the day the Lord and I got married (my concept of getting married to the Lord means agreeing to take a vow to be committed to Him for the rest of my life). I bought myself a promise ring, and every time I looked at my finger, it reminded me of the covenant I had with the Lord. I figured if He could make me His wife, it would be motivation to stay on track.

Unfortunately, I broke my wedding vows to Him. Even to the Lord I could not have been faithful. My good friend and sister in Christ could not make it to the wedding. She was a highly spiritual person, and I wanted someone to witness my commitment to God. The ceremony took place at three that morning. I chose that time because it was my favorite moment when we would spend quality time.

Of course, we need to worship Him in spirit and in truth. I am aware of that, but I don't think Jesus minded. If He did, He would have let me know that it was wrong. Part of the reason why I was so convicted was because of my vows with Christ. I learned later in my Christian walk that one should never make a vow to God that he or she cannot keep. I hated the fact that I allowed myself to be carried away foolishly and become deceived, but God always forgives sin. Maybe if I had meditated on 1 Peter 5:8, which says, "Be sober, be vigilant; because your adversary the devil, as a roaring lion, walketh about, seeking whom he may devour, my decision would have been different."

I lost my physical virginity at seventeen, but it meant nothing. I could not erase the image of the guy who took my second virginity. I was supposed to be saving myself for the Lord as He instructed me to do in the Bible.

I needed to feel the warmth of a man, his fingers caressing me and reminding me of how beautiful I was. I needed that reassurance. I gave God a few months of walking in sobriety, and I was ready for the mate He promised me. There was no way I was going into the New Year without being married. I needed God to send me a husband right away. When I saw that there was no potential for a husband, I regressed.

For years, sex had been my only means of escape; it was my opium. I used it to escape from my sorrows. There were challenges in life that I was afraid of confronting and sex was how I dealt with my issues. I thought it was impossible for God to deliver me because of my strong addiction to pornography and masturbation. I remember becoming so frustrated and having to pull over in a parking lot to satisfy myself in the middle of the day. I was an addict—there was no denying that. I enjoyed those moments of intense orgasm—moments when I could lose myself in the bliss of sexual fantasy.

I know a Christian has to deny such pleasure and confirm to the things that please God—and that was exactly what I was trying to accomplish. The Holy Spirit later revealed that part of the reason I was susceptible to falling was because I was no longer meditating on the word. I was becoming complacent and was dependent on myself and not of the things of God. I should have meditated on 1 Corinthians 10:13, which says, "There is no temptation taken you but such as is common to man: but God is faithful, who will not suffer you to be tempted above that ye are able; but will with the temptation also make a way to escape, that ye may be able to bear it."

The man I lost my second spiritual virginity to was not a Christian; he was a man of the world whose moral standing in regard to sex before marriage did not reflect the morals of God. His philosophy was that God is a forgiving God and would ultimately forgive all sins. He felt that sin was sin, and it didn't matter if you fornicated or stole a mango from a tree. This was the one guy I could not get out of my mind—I blamed him for my downfall.

When we met, I was shopping with a girlfriend. I made a joke and pleaded with him to buy me something nice. He laughed and continued talking. I did not think much of it, but when we went into one of my favorite stores, he paid for a couple of my items. My girlfriend was a little disappointed because she knew about my past struggles, and she was worried that I was stepping out of godly character. I assured her that it was okay. I had been faithful to God for almost a year, and she did not need to worry.

When we left the mall, he agreed to drive us home. We dropped my girlfriend off first and proceeded to my apartment. I felt an overwhelming feeling come over me. I found myself in the Enemy's trap. He pulled up to my apartment, and we walked inside. I figured that the sin would be less if there was no penetration.

When he left, I felt so guilty that I imagined the Holy Spirit saying, "If you repent from your sins and agree not to see this guy again, I will restore your purity. I will erase this as if it never took place."

I did so halfheartedly; I was torn between God and a man. I did what was right and deleted the guy's number from my phone. In less than five minutes, he called me. He wanted to see me again to talk to me about something. I opened the door and he walked in. We started talking—and then we ended up on my bed. We were about to kiss when his phone rang; someone on the other end said it was an emergency. He got dressed and left. I knew God had intervened, God was trying to prevent me from making a big mistake, but I was too blind to see.

Sin cripples your ability to see clearly. We spoke for hours on the phone that night—until three o'clock. I was using the time I usually allocated to God to entertain a man's lustful desires. He claimed that he had once walked with God—and wanted me to help him get back on track. His request somewhat took my guilt away. I consoled myself a little by thinking it was God's plan for me to help him get on track.

The next day, I brought my Bible to his house with the intention of converting his soul. That was the day I lost my virginity for the second time. No one was at his house and we sat in the living room talking about God. He shared sentiments about how he loved God and wanted so much to start going to church again. He arranged his music system and started to sing gospel music. He had such a melodic voice. I was very impressed that I was in the company of someone who at least was once friends with God.

He sang and I listened. He mentioned that I was very attractive, and he respected my religious views and would never do anything intentionally to cause me to jeopardize my relationship with Christ. He said he thought that it was perfectly normal to cuddle in bed. He asked me if I wanted to relax in bed and continue our conversation.

I should have read between the lines, but I was too wrapped up into the moment. I was forcing myself to remain in denial. I did not want to accept the moment for what it really was. I was not even a bit reluctant. When I looked into his eyes, they were genuine. The moment he left the room, I blocked any godly thoughts from my mind. Strangely, I felt the presence of someone standing at the foot of the bed.

"Father," I said, "I am sorry. I know you are disappointed in me, but I need to feel good. I need to enjoy myself for a change. I know it bothers you so please do me a favor and do not look."

I was really hoping that God would just look away. I knew my guilty conscience was playing games with me. It was like being intimate with a guy and having your father walk in—how embarrassing. I gave him a part of me that I was saving for the Lord. He saw the look on my face; I wish he felt the sadness that accompanied my heart. God had restored my purity, and I gave it away against His will.

The next day, I insisted that he destroy my number and we could never see each other again. He said that I was being very unrealistic and that he really could fall in love. He said that he felt used and we should at least remain friends.

In my mind, a woman using a man for sex seemed ridiculous, and I was not buying that. My heart began to grow cold and bitter toward him. For a month, I dodged his calls. I would peek through my door when he knocked and I'd refuse to answer. I avoided him on the street. As good as he was in satisfying my needs, he certainly was not worth throwing my relationship with Jesus down the drain.

One thing I learned from that experience was to never tempt God. If you know you are weak in a particular area, stay away from whatever it is that would cause you to fall. You are just as strong as your weakest link. It is not wise for women who are struggling with lust of the flesh to go on dates alone. Bring friends with you or get an accountability partner—someone that you can trust. Don't take the risk—it is not worth it.

I searched my heart that night, but I could not find answers to my big questions. What could I have done differently to prevent myself from giving in? I knew it was time to regain my dignity and self-control. I felt that if I did not act right away, it would be too late. As time passed, I began feeling even more sorry for myself. I needed to figure out why I had done what I did and try to implement a measure that would prevent me from doing this again. I decided never to be alone again with a male.

Because of my burning desire to please the Lord—but experiencing such failure—I was experiencing intense psychological pain. I felt like a failure; there were times when I felt like giving up. Moments from my past were often brought to life—the death of my mother and sister, being in jail, sleeping in my car, wandering hopelessly. The act of walking in total disobedience was more than enough to drive me insane.

Chapter 13

MY STRUGGLE TO REMAIN PURE as a Christian woman was not easy, but God delivered me 100 percent. I know because my mental approach toward sex has really changed. I guess He allowed me to experience certain failures so that I could be strengthened.

The Lord told me that He was going to deliver me in a dream and heal me from all emotional instability. He did. I spent a lot of my time reading psalms that contributed a lot toward my spiritual growth.

These are some of my favorite psalms that comforted me in moments of distressed.

Psalm 1 (whenever I am sad and need comfort):

1. Blessed is the man who walks not in the counsel of the ungodly, not stands in the path of sinners, nor sits in the seat of the scornful.
2. But his delight is in the law of the Lord and in His law he meditates day and night.
3. He shall be like a tree planted by his rivers of water, that brings forth its fruit in its season, whose leaf also shall not wither and whatever he does shall prosper.
4. The ungodly are not so, but are like chaff which the wind drives away.
5. Therefore the ungodly shall not stand in the judgment nor sinners in the congregation of the righteous.

6. For the Lord knows the way of the righteous, but the way of the ungodly shall perish. In Jesus mighty name. Amen.

I recite this psalm sometimes three times a day to ensure that I am always clean in the eyes of God. It is always important to repent of our sins before we get into the presence of God.

Psalm 51:

1. Have mercy upon me o God, according to Your loving-kindness, according to the multitude of Your tender mercies, blot out my transgressions.
2. Wash me thoroughly from my iniquity and cleanse me from my sin.
3. For I acknowledge my transgressions and my sin is always before me.
4. Against You only have I sinned and done this evil in Your sight that You may be found just when you speak and blameless when you judge.
5. Behold I was brought forth in iniquity and in sin my mother conceived me.
6. Behold You desire truth in the inward parts and in the hidden part You make me to know wisdom.
7. Purge me with hyssop and I shall be clean wash me and I shall be whiter than snow.
8. Make me to hear joy and gladness that the bones you have broken may rejoice.
9. Hide Your face from my sins, and blot out all my iniquities.
10. Create in me a clean heart, O God, and renew a steadfast spirit within me.
11. Do not cast me away from Your presence and do not take Your Holy Spirit from me.
12. Restore to me the joy of Your Salvation, and uphold me by Your generous Spirit.

13. Then I will teach transgressors Your ways and sinners shall be converted to you.

14. Deliver me from the guilt of bloodshed O God the God of my salvation and my tongue shall sing aloud of Your righteousness.

15. Lord, open my lips and my mouth shall show forth Your praise.

16. For You do not desire sacrifice, or else I would give it, You do not delight in burnt offering.

17. The sacrifices of God are a broken spirit a broken and contrite heart these O God, You do not despise.

18. Do good in Your good pleasure to Zion, build the walls of Jerusalem.

19. Then You shall be pleased with the sacrifices of righteousness with burnt offering and whole burnt offering then they shall offer bulls on our alter.

20. In Jesus' Mighty Name Amen.

Psalm 35:

1. Plead my cause O Lord with those who strive with me, fight against those who fight against me.

2. Take hold of shield and buckler and stand up for my help.

3. Also draw out the spear and stop those who pursue me. Say to my soul, I am your salvation.

4. Let those be put to shame and brought to dishonor who seek after my life, let those be turned back and brought to confusion who plot my hurt.

5. In Jesus mighty name.

Psalm 32

1. I will instruct you and teach you in the way you should go. I will guide you with my eye. Your heavenly Father

Chapter 14

I WAS VERY DEPRESSED WHEN I started a nursing program at a very small university, but I could not put my hands on the reason why. There were mornings when I would stay home from school. The few times I attended classes, I would sit in the back and fall asleep. Some of my classmates would tease me about my efforts.

A friend said, "Hermie, you are not making any effort at all. I know you are a smart girl. You can make it."

I know she was looking out for me, but I was not at peace. There were times when I would question God and ask Him if that was what He had intended for me to do. For almost a year, I did not get a clear response.

During the first semester, I wrote a letter to the head of the department, informing her that I wanted to change my major to social work. Two days later, some of my friends told me that I was crazy to do so. I sent her another letter stating that I changed my mind. A part of me just did not feel connected to the profession. I had no incentive to pick up my books or go to the labs. I hated going to clinicals.

My worst days were Thursdays when we had to go to the labs. I dreaded getting up in the mornings. Several friends said that I was not making any effort, and I should be glad that I had been accepted to the program because of its competitiveness. I agreed with most of them and decided to change my attitude.

For months I tried to find contentment in nursing—but the more I tried, the more my heart would feel dissatisfied. One night I was 100 percent delivered from fornication. (I knew I was delivered 100 percent because God had promised me that, and He had revealed to me in a dream that He would be doing it pretty soon.) The Holy Spirit guided me to look up Psalm 32 verse 8. I had no clue what this scripture was about, but I did as I was told because the Lord used a lot of the psalms to communicate with me.

The verse stated that God was going to guide me with His eyes. How fortunate was I to be guided by someone so powerful and mighty? I felt as if The Holy Spirit was saying, "It was not my intention for you to be a nurse."

I was shocked because I often had dreams of praying at a bedside for sick people. How could that be I questioned God? How could that be and why now? The Holy Spirit assured me that He had bigger plans for me and that I would never be happy as a nurse. He led me to go in and change my major. I started seeing myself more as a counselor going to jail, camps, and juvenile halls—helping people. I felt like the Holy Spirit told me that it was Him that had instructed me a year earlier to inform the department about changing my major, but I listened to my friends and disobeyed His request. He said that was why I was so bitter. I was led by the Holy Spirit to register for classes in my new major.

"Wow, Father; I have an outstanding balance owed to the school. How is that possible?"

I never needed to take summer classes because I had completed all my prerequisites and only needed to take the core classes and because summer classes were too expensive. In my mind, I was almost convinced that the Enemy was trying to make a fool out of me. Change my major and register for summer classes? That did not seem possible. I called one of my friends and discussed it with him. I said God asked me to change my major and sign up for summer classes. I mentioned that I owed the school over a thousand dollars and they were not going to let me take classes unless I paid or made arrangements to pay. Even if I decided to make a payment arrangement, how was I going to pay for those classes? I had never been offered financial aid. He told me to trust in the Lord.

I got dressed and walked into the business office. I felt led by the Holy Spirit to tell the woman that I owed money, but I had interest in taking classes. When I told her what my plans were, she said they could make arrangements, but I would have to talk to the head of the department. I left her office with a payment extension for the month of August, but I still was not satisfied because my concern was finding money for the summer class.

As I was heading out of the building, it felt like someone told me to walk over to the financial aid office and let them know that I wanted to take classes but I didn't have any money. The girl at the financial aid office greeted me with a smile and asked me for my ID number.

She researched my information and said, "You withdrew from one of your classes last semester and you were paid to attend this class. In situations like this, you usually have to refund the money that was given to you. I already knew that information, but I shook my head and said, "I agreed to pay the business office as soon as I can."

She told me that they could award me $2,300 for the summer. My heart was rejoicing when she said I was qualified. I don't recall her last words. I was just so relieved to know that the Holy Spirit was guiding me for real. I hurried out of the office and called my friend. "Babe, you would not believe this: the financial aid office gave me free money to do my classes."

I thank God and praise Him for coming through for me again. I felt peace in my heart. Changing my major was the best thing that happened to me. I would be graduating with a master's in social work. With all the experiences that would be gained as a social worker, God would definitely use me to impact people's lives.

I love people and I really want everyone to experience the Love of Christ. My goal is to be a radical for Christ, but I know God has to do a lot of work in me. I have so many areas that need improvement. The most important thing is that I am on the right track and I am doing what God has in mind for me. I often wondered what would have happened if I had decided to listen to my friend and not the Lord. The lesson here is to never allow people's opinions of what they think is best for you to be your indicator of what is right for you. Always seek the counsel of the Holy Spirit.

When God promised me a car, I had no money. I was walking in the snow to get to and from work. I had lost everything and I had to start all over. The fancy car I was driving had been repossessed. I no longer was depending on men to support me and it was very hard meeting my bills. I went from having lots of nice clothes to having three pair of shoes. The Holy Spirit told me that I was going to have a car on January 6—and it happened just as He promised. Someone put money in my account and I was able to buy an old car for cash. I have been driving it for two years and the only thing I ever had to do was change the oil. I have friends with newer cars who often break down, but my car has never failed me. When something is from God, it is really good. If God promises you a husband, just wait on Him. Trust God that the man will be a match made in heaven.

I started to write this book in the summer while taking my classes that the Lord had asked me to. He had blessed me and gave me so much favor and an earnest desire to learn. I ended with an A and the class was very interesting. God had truly blessed and rewarded me for being in His will. I have no regrets. I thank the Lord for guiding me with his eyes.

God's Plans for My Future

I have no problems sharing the plans God has given me for my future because I have faith and no one can steal my blessings. God had really proven Himself faithful to me and has granted me favor in the eyes of man. He gave me hope when my entire life was shattered. All I had was men who sexually exploited me. They took so much from me, but God restored my purity.

I don't masturbate. I don't fornicate. I am totally surrendered to God in that way. If I can do it, any other woman can too. Fornication is a spirit; it is not okay in the eyes of God. I have strong urges that hit me now and then, but God always provide a way out so I don't have to resort to sinning. I hope I never resort to fornication again, but I can promise that I will try my utmost not to ever put myself in a compromising situation with a man. If I feel like resorting to porn or masturbation before I yield to the hands of the enemy, I would cry out to Jesus and remind him of the promises He made to me. Psalm 17 says, "I will uphold your feet in my path so that your footsteps will not slip." I just have to trust on the Lord to direct my steps.

He told me that I was going to be married to a wonderful man who would love me for me. He told me that I was going to be financially stable. The Lord assured me that I would be impacting millions of people all over the world—and I believe Him. He said that all I have to do is seek Him first and everything would be handed down to me.

Sometimes when I talk to my heavenly Father, I let Him know how much I appreciate what He has done for my life. If He never does another thing, I am content—and I am happy. God delivered me from fornication. Never in my wildest dreams have I ever imagined being able to go without sex or even masturbation or looking at pornography.

The Holy Spirit is a trooper. He is a fighter. I am so happy He stood up for my help when everyone thought that I would never make it. Jesus said, "Yes, you can. My death on the cross will not go in vain."

Jesus delivered me from gossip. Folks who knew me back in the day could attest to the fact that gossip was my middle name. I was critical of everything. I was one of the folks who loved hearsay. Now my friends can say that I not only refrain from gossips, but I don't say anything behind anybody's back that I cannot say in their presence. Thank you, Lord.

I don't depend on men for anything; my source comes from the Lord. Do you have any idea how empowering this is for me? Daddy in heaven pays my bills. Yes, He does. I have become very confident in who I am. God knows that I had battled low self-esteem for a very long time. Can you believe that I am a woman of character now?

Before God delivered me, I lied about everything. Now I am the most honest person you will ever meet. I have developed a compassion for people; I don't even hate my enemies. God has delivered me from that too. No one should underestimate the true power of God. God's power is infinite. Most people make God out to be a monster, but He loves us tremendously and God's ways are not our ways.

When my mother died, I thought that God did not love me, but I was wrong. God knew everything was going to work out for the greater good. We need to stop accusing God when things do not go our way. God is supreme—He knows best. Whenever God places something in your heart, you need to do it. God instructed me one day to give a total stranger fifty dollars—and I did. Within two days, I received a scholarship for $1,100 that I never applied for. It was a miracle from God.

What Kind Of Man Do I Want My Husband to Be?

I know that my husband is spiritual man. God will never send me someone that I would be unequally yoked with. Since that is out of the way, here are some of the qualities I want in my husband:

- A nice sense of humor. I love to laugh, and I want my husband to be the same way.
- Honest—no lies whatsoever. I believe with the Holy Spirit guiding me, my husband and I can overcome any obstacle so we clearly have no reason to be dishonest with each other.
- Financially stable.
- Emotionally stable—no attachments from the past.
- Humble— I don't care how many blessings God put in His life, I want him always to treat other people with respect.
- Kind.
- Love his family.
- Educated—I want him to stimulate me intellectually.
- Open sexually—have no restriction toward pleasing me as long as it pleases God.
- Understands my personality and embraces me for me and does not try to change me—only God can do that. If you ask me, He is doing a beautiful job.
- Race is not a key factor.
- I want my husband to be very romantic. Flowers, candlelight dinners, beaches, sunsets, presents—the whole nine yards.

- I don't care about his past—as long as there is not any emotional attachment with anyone from his past. No baby mama drama.

My Advice to Gays/Lesbians and Adulterers/Fornicators

Guys, I love you, and God loves you. Stop making excuses. You were not born that way. God made you perfect in His eyes. Get a grip on your actions. Homosexuality and lesbianism are wrong. Men and women— even if you are just doing it to entertain your partner—cut it out. You can be delivered. I don't care if you are a man that talks, laughs, and dresses like a woman. God can bring you back to being a man again.

Believe me when I say I am not judging any of you because there was a time before I was walking in victory—before God delivered me—I had my share of messing around with women. I even made love with two men at the same time. I remember going to strip clubs and making out with women so my boyfriend would be entertained. I am not ashamed to admit it; it is the truth, but it is all in my past.

Please don't think I am judging you. God is the only judge. I was once walking in sin, just like Paul, but Jesus saved me. I experienced the love of Christ. I know how happy it feels to be set free. I want to help people all over the world. I did not write this book because I felt like writing. No—the Holy Spirit asked me to. I had lots of sex outside the context of marriage. I cheated in my marriages. I was once an adulterer. I have a police record. I have been to jail. But now, none of this matters. I am a new creature in Christ and the old things are passed away. I am confident about who I have become in Christ. It is my role to help others. Our lives belong to God and this behavior offends Him. I am not ashamed of my past because, when God looks at me, He sees a bright future and that what is what matters most. People of the world, go to God in prayer right now. In fact, repeat this prayer and ask God for deliverance.

> Heavenly Father, I am aware that I am walking in sexual impurities, please deliver me. I accept your son Jesus to come

into my life and I am truly sorry for my sins. Teach me how to overcome my sexual sins. In Jesus' mighty name. Amen.

Pick up your Bible and read it. Have a sincere heart. I believe we have to embrace each other because I was embraced by a lot of people who never judged me when I was in the world. A lot of people showed me love and I want to be able to do the same. Gays and lesbians, forget about the myths about being born that way. Just give yourself to God, and I will be interceding for you.

If you are a gay person in ministry and living on the down-low, please come out and be open about it. Don't worry about what society may think. The Bible said what it profits a man to gain the whole world and lose His soul.

One thing I learned in my Christian walk is to never cover up your sin. The main reason I was healed was because of my openness with the issues I was facing. I was not afraid to talk to my pastor, friends, or anyone.

God forgives and loves you. Who cares if a man chastises you? Guys, please do it for the sake of Christ. He died on the cross to save us from our sins. God loves people who are struggling with issues so He can show off His mighty power in their lives. Christian folks, let's not be critical of others. Let's offer them all the help and love they need. In case you are wondering if I am a preacher—I am not. I am just a beautiful woman who is filled with the Holy Spirit. I love the Lord and I know the Lord loves me—and I know the Lord loves you too. I don't have all the answers, but I do know God delivered me from sexual immorality and he is waiting to do the same for you.

To all the Christian women who are living with boyfriends, please stop it right now. You will never prosper in Christ if you choose to remain this way. Let me ask you a question. Answer me honestly. Would you like someone to walk into your house and ruin it? Well, that is exactly how the Holy Spirit feels. Remember that your body is the temple of God.

Letters Written to God

Please allow me to share some of my intimate letters that I have written to my heavenly Father.

On 12/29/09:

> Dear Father,
>
> I am trusting in You to provide for my rent. Lord, You said in Malachi 3:10, "Bring all the tithes into the storehouse, that there may be food in my house, and try me in this. Father, You said You open for me the window of Heaven and pour out for me such blessing that there will be not be room enough to receive it. In verse 11, you said, "You will rebuke the devourer for my sake, so that he will destroy the fruit of my ground. Nor shall the vine fail to bear fruit for me in the field." Father, I am trusting Your word. I took $42 from my rent and gave it to You. The weather is bad, and I am not sure if I will be able to work all assigned days. My dad promised me $100, you told me, Father, not to take it. Father, in the mighty name of Jesus, I am turning over my financial obligations to you. Father, I trust in You and in Your word. Thank You for providing all my needs. In Jesus' mighty name.
>
> Your daughter,
> Hermie

The Lord answered my prayer and my rent was paid—and I even had a little left over to shop.

On 12/26/09:

> Heavenly Father, in Jesus' name, I was just bothered by one of those demons. Father, in the name of Jesus, I command that dirty foul beast to depart from me in the name of Jesus. I am convinced that I am protected by You and You promised me no weapon against me shall prosper or stand. Father, I know You are very merciful and You don't take part in

wickedness. Father, today I ask you to destroy all wicked influences around my life. Please, Father, cleanse my spirit and my soul. Free me from all spiritual bondages. Father, in the name of Jesus, I loosen the Holy Spirit over my life to guide and protect me. According to Matthew 18:18, whatever I loose on earth will be loosed in heaven. Please cover me with the Blood of Jesus. Father, let your supreme power flow throughout the earth. Oh my King of endless worth. You alone are God. You are mighty and powerful and worthy to be praised. Father, last but not least—uphold my feet in Your path that my footsteps would not slip. I love you, Lord, and teach me to worship, praise, and love You with all my body, heart, and soul. In Jesus' mighty name. Amen.

On 2/26/10:

Father, I was a fool to think I could live a day without You being the priority in my life. I was a fool to let thoughts of evil near me. I was a fool for so many things I did wrong in Your sight, but, Father, I would be a greater fool if I don't return to You. Father, You alone have the key to my heart. Only You know my thoughts and desires. Father, only You can give me the inner piece that my heart and soul crave. You sent Your son Jesus, my Big Brother and Friend, to save my soul from a life destined for destruction. Oh my God of Abraham, Isaac, and Jacob. The only true and living God. Please stretch out Your arms and hold me. I need You now, please comfort me. Father, I know that I am not perfect, please forgive all my transgressions. Make me as white as snow. Father, please teach me how to remain in Your presence and follow Your precepts at all times. It is not by my will. Let Your will be done. In Jesus' mighty name.

On 3/29/10:

Father, Oh beautiful, merciful, kind and loving Father. In Jesus' name, I come into Your presence, please rescue my soul from sin. Father, I masturbated today. Oh how sorry I am.

Father, I am tired of sin; it is wearing me down. I am so tired of the urge to fornicate. I just want to keep my body Holy as the temple of God. Father, rescue my soul from destruction. Help me to be upright and sin no more. Father, I can do all things in Christ who strengthens me. Forgive me, Father, for all unrighteousness. In Jesus Christ's Holy name. Amen.

On 12/26/09:

Father, you have not given me a spirit of fear, but of power and of love and of calm and well-balanced mind and discipline and self control (2 Timothy 1.7) You said that there is power in Your word to equip me from bowing my knee in fear to the enemy's desire. I can do what God wants us to do, even if I have to be afraid.

On 12/23/09:

My Father, in Jesus' name, my heart goes out to You. I just want You to know that I appreciate You for all Your love patience, guidance, and protection. I keep asking myself where I would be if it were not for the Blood of Jesus. Father, You have been very good to me. I really want You to know that as long as I live, my soul will always thirst for You. In Jesus' mighty name. Amen.

On 3/26/10:

Father, I come before You today, because there is no one else to turn to. According to David, who do I have in heaven but You? Yesterday was very difficult for me. I let my guard down and gave in to the flesh. Father, I was hurting so badly. Instead of turning to You, I turned to a man to provide me with false comfort. Father, I yelled at you, and blamed You for my wrongdoings. Father, how wrong was I to treat You with disdain. Please, Father, I am asking You for Your help today. I have these overwhelming sexual desires and I resort to cycles of immorality. Father, it is so hard to control these urges most of the time. It is like something takes over and I just put myself in situations that compromise my promises to You. Deep down, I don't want to destroy the dwelling place of the Holy Spirit. Father, rescue my soul from death and my body from destruction. Teach me Lord to keep my body as the living sacrifice to You. In Jesus' mighty name. Amen.

On 10/20/09:

Today, Father, You have proclaimed me to be Your special person just as You promised me that I should keep all Your commandments. You promise that You will set me on High above all nations which You have made in praise in name and in honor. In Jesus' name.

On 11/26/09:

Dear heavenly Father, I can honestly say You are perfect. You are a darling. I love You. Thanks for loving me with such intensity. I love kissing Your cheeks. I love rubbing my fingers in Your hair at nights and early in the morning. I love my big brother and best friend. I don't think You could have asked for a better Son. I love you, Father. In Jesus' mighty name. Father, I shall not die but live to declare your works.

One of the things I am very sensitive to as a Christian woman is when a person tries to tell me that my experiences with God are not real. I hate that kind of remark. God chooses whomever He wants to communicate with just as He sees fit. I am a young Christian woman, with intense love for the Holy Spirit. I honestly believe that He is guiding me throughout life journey. Some people can be very jealous as to the manner in which God works in your life. As a young believer, I am often faced with that.

There are many times when the Holy Spirit leads me to pray for my enemies. I live my life based on faith; I don't think that there is anything that I cannot achieve. I was once hopeless, but God gave me hope. Why should I limit myself by putting my dreams and aspirations on the shelf? God is my source of strength; He is my help in trouble. I had lots of friends, but when I was in trouble, no one came to my aid. I was forgotten behind bars. If it were not for Christ, my sanity would not have been restored. I think it is crucial for Christians to be primarily concerned with a relationship with Christ and not get too caught up with other people's affairs. I have to remind my friends most of the time that God is not a respecter of persons. He doesn't care about your past—that is not important to Him.

One has to learn how to face challenges in life. I have had my fair share of disappointments, but during my difficult moments, I was never left hanging. God always provided a way out.

Intimate Moment with God

In case you are wondering why I have a strong desire to please the Lord, the truth is that the Lord and I have a unique relationship. He is my friend, my lover, my Father—he is my everything. He is the only person who understands me for me. He relates to me on my level. He knows when I need to be comforted. He knows I love a sense of humor; I often feel teased and the Holy Spirit puts a smile on my face whenever I am down.

I remember asking Him why He made me so short; my imaginative response was that it is easier to carry me on His back. I would imagine the Holy Spirit having a blast. The Lord enjoys showing off His power in my life—especially when I am going through financial problems. He would wait until two minutes before my phone would be disconnected before paying my bill. He would let me leave the house with an empty tank of gas, thinking I would break down on the way, but would provide the gas right before I set foot in the car. He would allow the bank to credit me over $200 in overdraft fees at a time when I needed money in my account. I could go on and on.

I spent more than eight years without a job; when I started trusting in the Lord, I was never out of a job. Depending on God to provide my needs is the best thing that could have happened to me. God has given me answers to test questions. He has allowed me to be highly favored in the eyes of professors. During my first semester in junior college, the dean of the school paid thousands of dollars for my tuition. It was a favor from God. I have watched God make my enemies favor me.

I am confident that whatever situation I am faced with, God will never turn His back on me. God always shows me the heart of someone so I know where I stand. I only have to say, "Father, in the name of Jesus, please show me that person's heart."

One week before I relocated, I was very sad. I did not have much money and I was uncertain of what was ahead of me. I knew God would provide, but I was doubtful. My heart was heavy; I wanted to cry out to my heavenly Father, but the tears would not flow. I was sad and just wanted to be comforted. "Please, Father, allow me to cry out to you."

The enemy was putting all sorts of stuff in my head—all the promises God made to me seemed so impossible. How was I to live for two weeks in a strange place with only rent money? I was at the point of feeling deserted. I guess I wanted Him to assure me that He would never disappoint me. I was living at Michelle's house. Michelle is the Christian woman who rescued me from being homeless. Michelle had a stack of gospel CD in her study room. I am never one to touch people's stuff without permission, but I felt as if the hands of God were leading me to the pile of about fifty CDs. I walked into the study and the Lord said number five. I grabbed the fifth CD and put it in the CD player. I was curious to find out what message the Lord had for me. The CD was not a gospel one—it was by Sade. I heard a voice again said number three. I put the CD on track three and the most beautiful voice said, "Listen to the words, babe. I am dedicating this to you." The words will blow your mind. I include the words of the song for those of you who do not know it. It sounded as if God was singing it to me.

"You think I'd leave your side baby, you know me better than that. You think I would leave you when you down on your knees. I wouldn't do that. I'll tell you you're right when you want. And if only you could see into me."

That was the Holy Spirit assuring me of His guidance and support. I listened to the song over and over. Whenever I feel down, the words comfort me. I know deep down that the Lord has a plan for my future—big plans.

When I was just a little girl, I knew that I would be somebody one day. I thought that I would win the lottery or marry very rich, but I never imagined being great in the Lord. Having the Holy Spirit guide me and reveal things to me. Who would have thought that God would do so much for a little girl like me? I came from a poor family. I had so many issues. I was addicted to sex. My God is an awesome God. I love Him.

I had many fights with the Lord, accusing Him of not loving me enough and telling Him how He favored men in the Bible. I guess I wanted His attention and I was going about the wrong way. I remember threatening Him to tear my Bible apart because I did not get my way with Him. If I could take back all the insults and obscene language that I directed to God even as a Christian, I would.

When I became more mature, God showed me that He did not mind. He forgave me and showed me that His mercy and grace were all over me. I would imagine the Lord saying, "Hermie, you are my darling. I would never be mad with you for long." Wow, that was comforting. He spoiled me—95 percent of the things I wanted, He gave.

There were times when I was asleep and would feel my heavenly Father caressing me. God knew how much I yearned for love and affection, and He provided it. When I started to mature in Christ, He was a bit sterner with me. He was still caring, but He did not allow me to have my way much. He would let me know the reasons why He denied my request because the things I requested were not right for me.

One day, I said, "Father, please tell me the one quality you love most about me. I know it is not about me, but I would just like to know." I was led to open up a book and the first word I saw was kindness. In spite of my past insensitivity toward men, I have a very kind, genuine heart. I am just like my mom was—I love to share and would give the shirt of my back.

The Lord taught me so many things. I don't know for certain where I would be without His guidance. I told Him that when I die, I want to sit on His lap and braid His hair in heaven. (I hope He has hair or at least grows some by the time I get to heaven). I told Him that I want to cuddle on His chest and read Him a story. (I haven't figured out what story I am going to read Him yet.) I imagined him saying, "Well, you may have to work really hard on earth and do everything right."

Call me insane if you like, but my relationship with God is my relationship with God. You create your own. I just get very excited and creative when I think of the Lord. The truth is that if it were not for my relationship with God, I would be in a mental institution. There was a time in my life when I lost everything—especially my hope and desire to live. When my mom died, I actually had a nervous breakdown. Just picturing her in that coffin is heartbreaking, but her dying thought me how to live. I can only hope and pray that she is in a better place.

I now have the desire to overcome all obstacles. God had given me strength beyond my capacity. He has developed character in me. I only wish that my family and friends—even my enemies—would turn to Him. A lot of people want to turn to God, but they don't want to part with their old ways. The Bible said what does it profit a man to gain the whole world and lose His soul. There is nothing in life more important that living for Christ. Mind you—it is not an easy task. I have encountered many days of frustration, but as I grow, God has equipped me to fight bigger and bigger battles.

My Childhood

I was ashamed of myself when I was growing up, but now I am proud of who I am. I remember knocking on my neighbor's door in the middle of the day and pretending it was my home. I had invited my friend Mary to visit me because I had visited her house frequently and she had demanded to see where I lived. I kept putting it off, but she grew tired of waiting and was beginning to think that I had something to hide. I was so relieved when no one was home. I knocked on the door and searched underneath the mat for a key that I knew was not there. I yelled, "How could Mom forget to leave the key?" I threw my arms up and down in fits of anger. I was so convincing that I had Mary believe that I was accidently locked out of my own house. She tried to console me by asking what I was going to do. I shook my head and rolled my eyes as if I had just come up with a brilliant idea.

Maybe I could go by my cousin house. I pointed to the old rotted board house that was leaning to one side. My brothers, sisters, niece, nephew, and our cousin were standing on the veranda. If she only knew that was where I really stayed, I would have died. I had so many friends in high school and there was no way I was going to risk losing them. I would have rather lied than lost my dignity. When my brother saw me, he knew that I was up to no good. He started talking to my other family members, telling them how to act in a manner that would not disgrace me.

I said, "Mary, let's go by my cousin's house and wait."

She looked at my house with pity. She said, "That is an old broken down house."

I smiled and agreed. I climbed up the broken steps and walked into the veranda. I shouted, "Did my mom leave the house key with you guys?"

I wanted to take Mary inside to show her the house. My cousin asked if I had looked under the mat. I had no doubt that Mary was convinced that I was truly living at my neighbor's house. It was getting late and my mom would be home soon. I was hoping and praying that my mom would not get home and expose my lie.

When it was time to leave, my brother gathered some ripe mangoes and handed them to Mary. He said, "I am sorry you did not get to see where Hermie lived. You would have like the inside of her house. She lives there with my mom and we live here because it is a lot of fun."

I looked at my brother and winked at him. I was signaling him to shut up in case he said something foolish. As we proceeded toward the junction, I heard my mom greeting one of her friends. My brother took off to warn her so she would not let out our little secret.

My mom was drunk; she approached my friend, gave her ten dollars, and said, "You must bring her back, Hermie, so she can see our house. Mary, next time you are coming, please let me know so I can stay at home."

Mary put the ten dollars in her purse and my brother and I accompanied her to the bus stop. My mom went home and threw herself on the floor.

She said, "Where is my food? I am hungry. Today Hermie brought her friend home and pretended that she lived in Mr. Church's house. I see no reason why she should be ashamed of where she lives. At least we keep our house clean."

My mom finished eating her rice and stew peas and fell asleep on the floor. My sister took a sheet and covered her legs. She drank to soothe the pain of rejection from men. I watched my mother being abused by men and wished in my heart there was something that I could have done.

I actually liked my mother drinking, she became very funny and easier to talk to. I don't think I would trade my mom for anybody else in spite of her addiction to alcohol. She was the sweetest person ever. My mom told me stories about how she became so depressed because she met a man and he broke her heart. She fell in love with him because he was a fighter; she saw him beat up a man in the village and was impressed. Although he had his finger chopped off in a fight, he never lost a battle. She said she had to sleep with other men to take care of the man she loved. Before he came into the picture, she was never a prostitute.

He used to take her to Chinatown. It was a place where prostitutes would meet and encourage her to sleep with foreigners for money. She said he would wait by the dock and, when she came out, he would be standing there with his hands all stretched out to receive the money. She said he was the main reason she started drinking heavily. He did not deny encouraging my mom to sell her body on the tourist boat, but he claimed that she would cheat on him in his face and bring other men to their house. He died in a vehicular accident when I was a teenager.

Over a period of time, I grew to resent him for how he mistreated my mother. As I grew older, and my eyes were opened, I began to see him for the manipulative person that he was. That evil man traveled and dumped my mother for another woman.

I remember my mom receiving letters from this woman whom she had never met. I quickly graduated from school and went on to teach with the intention of helping her with the bills. I watched my mom suffer as a result of some of her choices. Her actions affected me a great deal. I became very rebellious at an early age. I fought, I cursed, and I defied authority.

My sister was molested at the age of twelve. After the incident, no one ever mentioned it. My mom lived closed to another man who was in a much better position to take care of her financial needs. The next morning when we woke up, there was a group of neighbors all over our house. My mother was getting advice from her friends about what needed to be done. It was about eleven o'clock the morning, the sun was shining brightly and my mom kept us away from school. She said she needed to destroy my sister's school uniform because she had done something awful.

My sister was crying, and nothing has ever distressed me more than seeing my sister's face as her school uniform burned. When I asked my mom why she was burning the uniform, she told me that my sister was all grown up. Days passed and my sister was not allowed to follow us to school. She would stay at home to help clean and cook. Her friends and teachers would ask about her wellbeing, but there was nothing that could be done. Mom's mind was already made up.

Soon, my sister became pregnant with her first child. Mom encouraged her to have an abortion. We were never allowed to discuss my sister's pregnancy or why that measure was necessary. My sister became rebellious and would fight with my mother. I guess she hated my mom for the decision. At fifteen, my sister got pregnant again and gave birth to a son.

In my heart, I knew I had to make a difference in the lives of my family. I did not want to make the same mistakes as my mother. I tried very hard in school, and made many friends, but I knew my life was a lie. I buried myself in a fantasy world and read books to escape from reality.

My mom did not demand much from me. She said she trusted that I would not do anything to bring shame unto her. I was allowed to attend carnival and go everywhere I wanted with her permission. She was protective of me in an unusual way, but I was empty.

At the age of seven, I was molested. I do not remember the details, but I know that God healed me from the resulting emotional tremors. I don't remember if he penetrated me. At the age of ten, I was touched appropriately by a much older guy; he used to touch his private parts and masturbate in my presence. He would touch my legs and other parts of my body. I remember him carrying me into the bushes and letting me see him pleasure himself. I would often watch with curiosity. I never felt the urge to tell my mom; after all, he never penetrated me. Whenever we were bathing in the yard, he would peek and make rude jokes at us kids.

My mom knew the guy was a pervert and confronted him one day. She never asked me whether or not he touched me. My mom had a very unusual way of dealing with things. I remember when I got my period at the age of twelve, she asked, "Are you sure it is your period and you were not molested by someone?"

I told her that I had not been as if she was quite wrong for asking me that. I love my mom—and I grew less and less ashamed of her as the years passed. She became my friend, but she was never someone I could confide in. Whenever she got drunk, she would spill your business out in the street. I think that is where I got my openness from. I never felt the need to keep any part of my life a secret.

She explained details of her life to me; I was born prematurely, weighing 2 pounds 11 ounces and she stole me from the hospital. The doctors did not think I would have made it. But my dad was very determined to have me live. My mom did not want me when I was a baby; she already had eight kids. She would leave me at home with my dad for him to fend for us. He burned charcoal and worked hard to take care of me. My mom told me that three other men had claimed me as their daughter and she was confused about who my real daddy was at times. I found out later that she had said the same thing to my two brothers. Nevertheless, my dad took very good care of us kids. I love my mom much more than I would even begin to love my dad. I believe she did what she did in life because she was lacking real spiritual guidance. She was a kind, beautiful woman. She might have messed around in her days, but I am quite certain that the Holy Spirit brought her to a place of repentance. If I had to live my life over again, I would not trade her for the world.

Night Tremors

I often had nightmares about a man turning into a ghost and molesting me. In one dream, I was in his living room. I was afraid to sleep in my room because I would hear voices laughing and footsteps all over the house, and we were alone in the house. That night I decided to sleep in the living room because I was very scared. In my dream, someone was strangling me. I felt a strong force over me and I started to fight. I could see blurry images and hear voices on the television. The force was trying to strangle me.

I cried, "Jesus, Jesus, help me," and I woke up. For many nights, I would be tormented by this dream. I agreed that that the enemy was using my mind to scare me at night. As days passed, the attacks became more real, and I would see him climbing the walls. It always happened when I was asleep. To prevent people from thinking I was mad, I buried it deep within.

In order to defeat those night terrors, God had to deliver me. I had to renounce every sexual sin and forgive every person that had ever hurt me in order for God to truly work in my life.

I will never forget the day that my mom wanted to kill herself; she came home drunk and was arguing with some of my relatives. She climbed up a tree and took a rope and said it was going to be her last day. In my young mind, I thought it would be a good idea in the sense that she would not have to endure any more pain. She climbed the tree, and tied the rope to a branch. My brothers were crying. I stared at her in the tree, but not a tear came to my eyes. I knew she was hurting and I thought she was doing the right thing.

When my older brother climbed the tree and cut the branches, she fell to the ground and threw up. As the days progressed, I watched mom separate herself from us on a more regular basis. She was hardly ever around.

My earliest memories of going to school included no one playing with us; being a Rasta was accompanied by much stigma. It was not until my mom decided to cut my hair cut that any changes occurred. Our house was old and rotted. It had one bedroom, a living room, and a kitchen. There was no inside plumbing. We had a pit latrine not too far away, but most of the time my brothers and I would defecate in the river and wash ourselves with the water. We would usually carry water from the river or from our neighbor's pipe to do our laundry and the dishes. We had no electricity.

I did all my reading in the daytime—and the nights were gruesome. Our house was isolated and surrounded my bushes. Owls and voices would appear after midnight. I often suffered panic attacks and developed a phobia for darkness. Very seldom, I would be invited to sleep over at my mom's house, but even there things were scary. She would get up in the middle of the night and scream that there was a cow trying to kill her.

My mom was not a religious person, but she believed in God in a funny way. She prayed to Jesus, but she performed a lot of rituals that were not of God. She was the one who taught me to how to pray at a very early age. She would say, "Hermie, whatever you do, never forget to pray in the name of Jesus."

I honestly felt that my mom knew the right thing, but she did not have the courage to walk in faith with Christ Jesus.

Letters to God

These were some of the most powerful letters I wrote to God during my struggle with the flesh:

> Dear Father, I don't know why You have found favor in me; after all, I have always let You down. I have made You promises upon promises. Not one have I kept. Father, deep down I want to do the right thing. But temptations and lustful desires keep getting the better part of me. Father, I not only messed up with a Muslim man, but two days ago, I was in bed with a man that was married. Father, there is a part of me that is hurting; believe me, I am hurting really badly. I am afraid that You will give up on me and one day You will realize that I am not good enough to be called Your daughter. Father, I want to ask You for a second chance, but I am afraid. Fear is slowly beginning to creep in. I am most afraid that I am going to mess up again. Father, my body is being consumed with sexual urges. It is becoming so hard to

control. All it takes is for me to be alone with a man and I feel the overwhelming urge to give in. Father, how could You respect someone like me, someone who has no character, someone so easy to throw her body to the dogs. Father, I don't want to continue living like this. I need Your help. Oh God, what am I doing so badly that is preventing me from keeping my promises to You? Father, if I was fighting in my strength please teach me how to fight in Your strength only. Teach me how to be faithful. Father, please teach me how to resist sexual temptations. Most importantly teach me how to love You with all my mind, body, and soul. I cannot sit there and make you another promise. Father, I am just going to ask for Your forgiveness. I am going to ask You to create in me a clean heart and teach me how to abstain from sexual immorality. Thank you, Father, for answering my prayer in Jesus' name. Amen.

I always find a sense of relief after I cry out to God. It is like my heart is filled with an instant peace. I know God wants what's best for me and I was determined to make the necessary commitment to God. I had to act quickly; I had to cease every ounce of communication with a male. I had to get rid of everyone who seemed to compromise my walk with Christ.

That morning, my hormones were acting up. I wanted so much to be in the arms of someone, but I know God would never understand. He had already told me that sin should never have dominion over me. He showed me that I did not yet know how to find happiness in Him. He was correct. The emptiness I felt inside saddened me.

"Oh God," I cried. "I know the promises You have made to me, and I am not going to ask you for something that I am not ready for. Please, Father, give me the strength to find happiness in You."

It I realized how dependent I was on men for my happiness. I chose to become celibate because of my undying desire to please God. To me, there is nothing more satisfying than saving yourself for your husband. "Nevertheless to avoid fornication let every woman have her own husband let the husband render to the wife due benevolence: and likewise also the wife to the husband" (Corinthians 7:2–3).

I have always been fascinated by being married. I've watched my mother struggle with men all her life. She had eight kids and no husband. I knew that I was destined to make a difference. I was going to be married before I had kids. I was going to be married to a wonderful man who loved me and the kids uncontrollably. Sadly my life did not work out the way I had hoped.

By the age of twenty-three, I had been divorced twice. I selected these men out of loneliness and I wanted someone to come home to me at the end of the day. As I grew older, my dependency on men escalated. I always had a man. Men were my God; they provided everything. My battles were with God and the flesh. This book will give readers a keen insight as to the power of God. God took me out of a life characterized by sin. I was drowning in a pool of disappointments. God came in and rescued me just in a nick of time. I knew I would be the woman He intended me to be.

I just wish I did not have to fight those urges. Please, God, take these urges away from me. The enemy would sometimes confuse my mind, convincing me that masturbation was okay, and I would occasionally give in. I would often download pornography on the Internet even though I did not really need it. I knew exactly how to satisfy myself, but I guess the enemy has a way of convincing you that you can never be satisfied. Most of the men in my relationships were addicted to pornography.

Pain/Death of Sister

After my second divorce, I was very empty. I began dating around, hoping to find someone to satisfy my emptiness. I was heavily medicated. I took Lexapro and other antipsychotic pills. My heart was mourning the loss of my sister. She died at the young age of thirty-five. She left six kids behind. The youngest was a few months old. Her death was unexplainable. The last conversation I had with her was weeks before she died. She said take care of myself—and that was the last I ever heard of her.

I blamed God for her death; no one saw it coming. A well-known psychologist on TV had contacted me to be on his show after receiving my letter. I guess he wanted to help me. I changed my mind because I did not want the publicity. I did not want the world to know what my issues were. My sister was admitted to a mental asylum after she was hit in the head with a stone by one of her classmates and was not able to function properly. She never learned how to read or write and would have to resort to putting an x as her signature. Memories of my sister with her chest open still haunt me today.

One day, I almost overdosed on pills. I had just left the therapist office. I went to discuss my hallucinations with her. She gave me 40 mg of a pill that was supposed to be started at 10 mg. I almost died driving home, but God rescued me. He sent angels to protect me on the road. I told God that I was going to do anything within my power to pursue happiness—even if it cost me my life. I wanted to find inner peace—the kind that I heard people talking about.

I often felt that God has His chosen folks and I was not one of them. I would sometimes imagine what it would be like to be a Christian, but I would either have to get married for a third time or give up sex—and I was not willing to do that. I continued to live my life with no direction. I did whatever I wanted—and I enjoyed every moment of it.

My Life in a Nutshell

Before I became a Christian, I was miserable. I was ashamed of myself and wished I was different. I hated my height; I was one of the shortest in my class. I wore heels to compensate for my height. I hated the fact that I grew up in a poor environment. My parents never really went far in school. Although my mom was very smart, she dropped out at a very early age. I would have died if any of my friends knew where I lived during my high school days. I hated the way I was labeled in high school. People teased me about my family and the fact that one of my sisters was always in trouble with the law. I had no stability in my house. I did whatever I wanted.

There were times when I begged her to stay, especially to sleep with me at nights, but 90 percent of the time, she refused. I don't remember getting a hug or being read a story before bed as they did on TV. I craved attention growing up. I would get in trouble in school just to be singled out. All the teachers knew me in high school, not because I excelled in class, but because I was a troublemaker. I would purposely pick fights just to be called into the principal's office. One day, I was planning to burn down the school. One of my best friends decided to meet at the science lab and start the fire. I walked three miles to the school and waited for hours, but she never showed up. The next day, I found out that she had moved to another state for good.

I hated walking in the mud during rainy season. I hated not having any privacy at home. I shared a one-bedroom house with eleven family relatives. There was no space to do anything. We practically lived on top of each other. When my grandmother died, I was so relieved to finally get a spot on the bed that she occupied with my sister and three nieces. Sometimes I would use my school uniform as a sheet to cover myself during the rainy season. I hated bathing in buckets outside the house, exposed. I hated my life—I wanted so much to escape. I always imagined getting married to a rich man. I went with older guys not because I was attracted to them, but because they were the ones who seemed more stable. If a guy did not have anything to offer, there was a 100-percent guarantee that I would never give him the time of the day.

Most of the men I dated provided me with financial stability. I cannot remember dating a guy and being in need of anything financially. At eighteen, I met a very nice guy from another island and instantly fell in love. Our relationship lasted a year after I found out that he was getting engaged to another woman. I was pregnant at the age of nineteen, but kept the pregnancy a secret from everyone and later had an abortion. When our relationship ended, I was devastated. I was really in love with him and he had promised to marry me. His disappointment caused me to resent men even more. I decided never to be faithful to a man under any circumstances.

At twenty, I was in total control of my life. I called the shots in my relationships. I dumped who I wanted to dump and I played who

I wanted to play with. I used men for money and never took anyone seriously. I always had another guy on the side in case the relationship did not work out. I would hurt a man's feelings for no apparent reason other than I feared he would hurt me first. I had a small desire for converting my life, but I did not think God would forgive me for all the evil things I had done and the lies I had told to get things my way.

I felt that I was being punished for my evil deeds. I hated God because I was raised to believe that He was a man. Although I hated my life, I never hated my family. We would cuss and fight each other, but we would never forsake each other in a time of needs. We stood up for each other whenever it was necessary. My brothers would fight and protect us—and my sisters would fight and protect my brothers if they had to. My mom was also known as a fighter.

I don't remember ever losing a fight in primary or high school, but when I grew older, I lost a lot of battles to girls who were far stronger than I was. I knew that a change would one day be necessary in my life. I knew that I would have to make a decision to refrain from my evil ways. Positive things were not happening for me. I was getting into lots of trouble. I found it difficult to maintain a relationship with a male— except my brothers—and would often sabotage my relationships with men who claimed to love me.

Although my heart was desperate to find love, I was also very afraid of receiving love. To be with me, a man had to possess a great deal of aggression. I loved a man that would hit because that is what I knew growing up. I witnessed my mother's black eyes. I saw blood running down her nose because she had been hit too hard by her boyfriends. Back in the day, it was perfectly normal—it was a prerequisite for being in love.

Haunted

My biggest problem was not being able to sleep at night. The demons were everywhere. In my heart, I was afraid. They would walk around the house at nights and torment me. I would leave the house and go in front of the supermarket to sleep under the streetlight. I needed to be safe.

One night I was in bed and felt a strange feeling. I saw a dark piece of cloth hanging in front of me and heard a voice tell me to take it. I extended my hand to snatch the cloth, but it disappeared. I got out of bed sweating profusely. I was so afraid. In my mind, I was being reminded of the scripture that says, "No weapon against me shall prosper or stand." The words were comforting, but I was afraid.

Two weeks later, I had to leave my home. Again I confronted homelessness. My car provided a place to stay. I was contented. Claudette, a beautiful woman of God from the Faith Center Ministries, gave me money for food and gas. One day I was walking in the church and a woman name Michelle came up to me and said that she needed to talk to me. She said that God told her that she must take me in to live with her. I was relieved. It was the best three months of my life. I was safe. I would imagine angels sitting on their doorsteps, protecting us at nights. For the first time, I felt safe. I no longer had to park my car on the opposite side of my school. I would drive to the gym at six o'clock in the morning and take a shower. I was working in the social sciences department and was often commended for being to work on time. No one knew that I did not have a place to stay.

Help from a Spiritual Leader

Thank God I was able to get a lot of help from my pastor. He was the kind of person who lived a very humble life. He was kind and genuine and never for a second was judgmental. I remembered walking into his office for counseling. There was always someone in the office besides us; he was indeed an honorable man. He was precise and used the Bible as the basis for everything. I know that I would not have been able to walk in such victory if the Holy Spirit did not direct me to him. The Lord promised that He was going to send people into my life to help me along the way. There was no doubt that this pastor was one of them. I am sharing some of these letters with the hope that they will be as much of a blessing to you as they were for me.

Dear Pastor

I am so happy that you are an approachable person because I really want to talk to you about an issue that matters to me. You are a great pastor; you seem genuine and you preach great messages. Among your many sermons, you spoke about putting God first, obeying the voice of God, etc. However, my concern is how I can incorporate everything you say into my daily living, which I know is your intended hope for all of us, especially when the problem that I am facing is never addressed.

It is my hope that this letter conveys the true meaning I want it to express.

You mentioned today that the church prepares us for challenges in the real world, so I was wondering, what help can I get to battle my struggle with sexual immorality. I am aware that my body is the temple of God and all that great stuff. I am aware that fornication is a sin. I am pretty much acquainted with a lot of the scriptures that speak about keeping one's body holy. The point I am trying to make is that I need to hear something a little more practical, and something I can easily relate to without feeling condemned.

I really appreciate your help on this matter. Thank you kindly.

Yours respectfully,
Hermion
6.27.10

Hermion, first of all, thank you for your honesty and for seeking God's solution to your problem. I know it is not easy to open up about personal problems. Also, please understand that you are not alone in your struggle. With so many sexually explicit images and messages thrust upon us every day, many struggle with maintaining pure thoughts and actions. In such a sexually charged environment, keeping one's self pure seems impractical and in some cases, undoable. However, from the onset, let me say it loud and clear, our God is bigger than any problem we have and is able when we are not! You are not without hope! From your e-mail I am not sure if you are struggling with sexual "temptation" (thoughts) or with yielding to sexual temptation (fornication). Since they are both sinful, I will address the issue from both perspectives. As you are being honest and open with me, I will be open and honest with you. Once we have crossed the road into sexual immorality (or any other sin for that matter), there is no "easy road back." That is why God told us not to do it in the first place. In doing so, He is not trying keeping us from something good; instead, He is preventing us from defiling our own bodies, or worst, from contracting some incurable sexually transmitted disease. Additionally, fornication does not only defile our bodies but also the body of the one whom we inappropriately give our self. God, who created sex and sexual desire, intended sexual intercourse to be an intimate relationship between a husband and wife. When sexual desire is prematurely awakened and cultivated outside the marriage relationship, the result is sex without intimacy or love. It is just sex for the purpose of fulfilling the fallen nature. Furthermore, sex outside of marriage typically results in devaluing of one's self-worth, perpetuates feelings of guilt and self-condemnation, and distorts one's understanding of true love. Moreover, sexual immorality is not about sex at all but about being accepted. Some see sex as a way to be "loved and accepted," when just the opposite is the case. After the pleasure is gone, there is an overwhelming since of shame and regret. Frankly, it is not possible to sin and avoid the consequence of that sin. As a believer, you must believe that you are already accepted in Christ. You are already precious to God, the Father. Therefore, preserving your body in a pure state is not an option. Having said this, there is a way back if you are willing to seriously apply the word of God to your situation. However, your struggle is exacerbated because you don't believe the word of God is practical or relevant to your situation. If you are to conquer this thing, then you are going to have to reverse your thinking and rely on the practicality of the word of God to see you through. There is no other way. Here are a few biblical-based suggestions to get you started. (1) Don't place yourself in situations where you are sexually tempted (1 Cor. 5:9–11). (2) Don't listen to sexually suggestive music or watch sexually suggestive movies (Matt 6:22). (3) Don't dress in a manner that is sexually provocative, for when you do, you are saying to every guy out there, I'm available— at minimum, you are planting inappropriate sexual thoughts in their mind, which is worse (Luke 17:1–2, Prov. 7:10–23, 2 Tim 2:9–10). (4) When you find yourself fantasizing about someone in sexual ways, immediately recognize that such thoughts come from your fallen nature and therefore are ungodly; immediately confess your sinful thoughts to God and replace them with the word of God (1 John 1:9). I believe your heart to be tender toward the Lord, or else you would not have reached out in this way. It is obvious that the Holy Spirit prompted you to do so. Therefore, know that God has not condemned you; neither do I. Instead, He is showing you how you can overcome and have the victory in this struggle, if only you will accept His way. I hope that you find this advice helpful. If we need to discuss this further, don't hesitate to e-mail me or call me at the office. Now "look unto Jesus, the author and finisher of your faith!" to see you through. God bless and strengthen you.

Hermion, Let me start by saying this. If you are a born-again believer, then you cannot be possessed by demons. It is not possible. This is not to say that your dreams are not real, but it is to say that they are not the result of demon possession. Jesus is very clear about this when He promises, "If the Son therefore shall make you free, you shall be free indeed" (John 8:36). Succubus and Incubus are both mythological figures, generally associated with witchcraft, sorcery, and pagan religions. The myth alleges that these supposed demons visit women at night in order to impregnate them and bear them demonic children. That is ludicrous! Spirits (good or bad) are sexless and incapable of having sex with humans (Matt 22:30). Therefore, they are incapable of reproducing themselves. False teachers attempt to link this myth to the Bible by quoting Genesis 6:2. But there is no biblical link whatsoever to this pagan myth (superstition). Having said all of that, it does not mean that your dreams are not real, as far as dreams go. Now read this slowly, the dream appears to be real, but there is absolutely no reality to the dream. The dream is no more than a figment of the imagination. Because it is rooted in our imagination, it can have physiological effects on our body (e.g. arousal). What you are really experiencing in your dreams are the consequences of prolonged promiscuity, pornography, and fascination with your own body. You are actually experiencing symptoms of withdrawal from sexual addiction. Your prolonged fascination with sex as a means of finding approval from men has saturated your mind with ungodly sexual thoughts (both day and night). Now, as you seek to replace those ungodly thoughts with godly thoughts, the old man is resisting because he (she) is accustom to being indulged. Like a drug addition, your physical body is experiencing withdrawal because, as a born-again believer, you are denying it that which before you so completely yielded. As a born-again believer, we must start believing and obeying the word of God and not the lies that come to from the old nature. For example, Romans 12:2 speaks of "renewing your mind." Romans 8:6 exhorts us against being "carnally minded." Ephesians 4:23 commands us to "be renewed in the spirit of your mind" and to "put on the new man, which after God is created in righteousness and true holiness." Faith demands action on our part. We must tear ourselves away from the old life and the deeds of the flesh (Rom. 8:13) and to embrace the new life that is in Christ. This does not happen automatically. We must "fight the good fight of faith" (1 Tim 6:12). In other words, recognize your dreams for what they are, the works of the flesh (Gal. 5:16, 19–21), take responsibility for the consequences of your actions (1 John 1:8–10), and, by the power of the Holy Spirit, purge yourself from those thoughts. "And every man that hath this hope in him purified himself, even as he is pure" (1 John 3:3). Hermion, it is *not* Incubus or Succubus that is causing your dreams, simply because they do not exist. Instead, the true source of your dreams is lingering thoughts from your old life trying to creep back into your new life. You must then acknowledge that fact, confess it to the Lord (e.g. "Lord I have brought this horrible thing upon myself, by not believing in you. Have mercy on me and strengthen me to win this battle."), and then "fight the good fight of faith! Now, I must ask you if you were molested as a child. If so, you must free yourself from that as well. How? By forgiving the molester(s). You may find this hard to do because it feels like you are letting the offender off the hook scot free. But the reality is that you will be freeing yourself from the anger, shame, resentment, and bitterness that have led you to do what you have done with your old life—use sex to find approval from men and women. Last, don't isolate yourself. That is the worst thing that you can do. Isolation will only make matters worse. You need to be in church where you can be strengthened in the Lord by being fed a wholesome diet of God's Word. As long as you isolate yourself, you are not only "giving place to the devil" in your life (Eph. 4:27) but more so, it is disobeying God's commandment to "not forsake the assembly of yourselves together as the manner of some is" (Heb. 10:25). You cannot fight this thing alone. We are here to help! As I close, please know that I appreciate your courage. It is not easy to open yourself up, as you have done. However, it is the only way to break free. Stay encouraged. Pastor

As I have said, I don't think that I would have achieved that level of maturity had it not been for the support I received at church. There is no doubt that he was a very spiritual man. He loved and cared so much about people. I poured out my heart to him and he assured me that God loves and forgives me. He arranged to have his wife, a very kind and down to earth woman, mentor me. He gave me a book called *Every Young Woman's Battle* by Shannon Ethridge and Stephen Arterburn. That book brought me instant healing. For months, we went through it. I discussed aspects of my life that needed healing and his wife prayed and advised me on ways to improve myself. We started meeting once a week, but then it went to two times per week. It is strange how God can use the people whom you least expect to bring healing to your life.

I was invited to this church by a friend of mine. When I walked in the building, I was not really feeling it. My church in my hometown had about one hundred people and here I was sitting in the congregation with about thirty folks. I looked around and not one man was in sight. *Wow,* I thought, *what had I gotten myself into?* I knew I was not ever going back.

The pastor spoke and about a few things that piqued my interest. I was impressed; that Sunday evening, I was invited to a member's home. She was a beautiful woman in her early sixties. She was hospitable and treated us like her own kids. I continued going to the church and was invited to the pastor's house for a surprise birthday party. When my friends and I walked in, I felt the presence of God all over. The house was very clean and I saw the way he treated his family and was very impressed. His family respected him quite a lot and I felt so welcome.

My association with the family brought me so much healing. I emulated their godly characteristics quite a bit and soon I was transformed into a beautiful woman with moral character. He taught us about morality, and how a young woman ought to conduct herself. I did not know that a woman's attire had such an impact on her spiritual growth. I always thought that God cared much about the heart and not the outside. The more I attended the church, the more I saw God working through me. There were times when the enemy was playing on my mind to quit, but God always convinced me that I was making a big mistake. The pastor was concerned about my salvation so I decided to accept Christ again in my heart that moment. I was granted instant deliverance from God was during that moment.

Delivered from Masturbation

God has completely taken away all my urges to masturbate or view pornography. He gave me the desire to say no to sexual temptations. He has restored my hope and blessed me tremendously. I have a reason to be happy. The Holy Spirit taught me how to love myself and not settle for less. God showed me His love in abundance. He was patient and kind in dealing with me. He loved me regardless of my mistakes. I am crazy. Yes, I am crazy in love with Jesus. I have met a lot of young women who have been battling the same issues as I have, and I would like to take the opportunity to let them know that preserving their body as a holy temple is doable. We can do all things in Christ who strengthens us.

If a man loves you, he will wait. I have had men tell me that they would have respected me more if I had not been so quick to give up the goods. I was thinking that I was doing them a favor, but the truth was that the best way to gain respect is to respect yourself. A man treats you how you allow yourself to be treated. Women enter into a relationship hoping that we will charm a man with our bodies, but think again. Sex is an important part of a relationship, but the best sex in the world cannot keep a man. I think real men demand much more. I am not an expert on relationships, but the truth is that experiences taught me well.

If I ever had to start my life over again, I would not make the same mistakes. You cannot change the past, but you can change your mental attitude toward it. Ladies, we need to find our own identity through Christ. All my life, I have been searching for happiness. I have tons of broken relationships and broken hearts—and not one man was able to fill the void. I got married to a man I only knew for two weeks because I thought that marriage was going change a lot of things.

Never place your hopes for attaining true happiness on a relationship. Only God can satisfy that empty void. Never go into a relationship because you feel lonely. Loneliness is a terrible disease; you can end up settling for less. Never think it is okay to put up with a man that cheats. A man that cheats on you with other women is very insecure about himself. If a man can expose you to diseases, he is not worth sharing your life with. You want a man that has something to lose—someone that would not want to jeopardize his relationship with God for anything. If he has a fear for God, he will treat you with respect and love you with his whole heart. God must be first in his life. If a man does not think that it is okay to wait until you are married to have sex, let him walk. Never have sex ought of obligation—wait until the time is right.

Ladies, never go out of your way to please a man. I know it may sound selfish, but most men do not appreciate a good thing. You have to constantly keep going above and beyond to satisfy his needs. To me, that is not healthy. Work within your parameters; do only what you are capable of doing. It is better for women who are trying to embark on careers to date men who have similar goals. I am not trying to be prejudiced, but I have learned from experience that when you have to lower your standards to accommodate a man, it always backfires.

I must let you know with 100 percent certainty that you cannot overcome any insecurity and achieve greatness without Jesus. It is impossible. When I was trying to overcome pornography, I would look on the Internet for resources that would decrease my sex drive. I would bathe with lime and try to incorporate lime in my diet because, from a young age, I was told that lime could cut your nature. Hey, that is working in your strength only. Such a strong perverse spirit needs only to be broken through Christ and Christ alone.

One of the things that God had to show me is to never think that you are too strong to fall. Stay away from tempting situations. Let's face it, if you know you are weak when you are around men, avoid situations that will cause you to compromise your relationship with God. Stay away from their homes—especially if no one else is around. Don't just kiss—it always leads to deeper things. Please, women, if you are going to walk the walk of saving yourself for Christ, you cannot even kiss. You cannot allow yourself to be aroused by any man unless you are married.

Engagements can be broken; please don't give up the goods to your fiancé. Women need to be in control of our lives; we are beautiful creatures, and God loves us and made us this way for a reason. The best gift we can give to Him is our body—that is where the Holy Spirit lives. How will you feel if your home was infested with rats? Imagine how the Holy Spirit feels when we exploit ourselves through sex. Ladies, God is good, don't beat yourself up if you find yourself struggling to keep your legs closed. Rome was not built in a day. One of the things that Jesus taught me is that as long as you want to be delivered, it will happen. Don't put a time line on it, only God can. Please, Christian ladies, don't cover up your actions. Don't sneak Tom and Fred inside your house and think nobody knows—God knows. He will expose you.

I remember sneaking a guy into my bedroom one day; my roommates were not around, and I was experiencing a fallen moment. God was so mad with my decisions that He totally caused the guy to experience erectile dysfunction. I was mad, but the guy was embarrassed. I never forget the look on His face when He could not get his groove on.

As the type of person I am, I was not going to sit there and pretend it was okay. I know it was insensitive, but I laughed in his face and accused him of wasting my time. He tried to make all types of excuses, but deep I knew it was God who did that. By the way, that was the straw that broke the camel's back. That moment brought me instant deliverance. That moment proved to me that God really wanted me for Himself and that I had to look at the bigger picture.

I remember sneaking out on a date with a man that I had no business going out with. As I stood by the gas station waiting for him, I heard the voice in my heart telling me to go home. There was no way I was going to turn back. My ride was going to be there in a few minutes. The guy picked me up and we drove to the restaurant. I was feeling so much guilt. I felt as if the Holy Spirit was sitting with us the entire time, protecting me.

Whenever I told people this story, they were shocked. Don't place any limitation on the Lord. He is God of the impossible. Everything the Lord told me came to pass. I believe in Him and I am not going to let people's opinions deter me from living my life based on faith. I have seen the miracles He has done for me and I don't need anyone to come between me and my relationship with God.

I was once living in the world, and Jesus cleaned me up very nicely. The Lord takes an interest in every aspect of my life. When I am sad, the Holy Spirit always finds a way to comfort me. The Lord was really patient with me and He will be with you too. In spite of my struggles to keep my body pure, I knew it was wrong and my heart was crying out to

God. I would cry, "Please Father, deliver me from sexual sins." I wanted to be purified and I never gave up praying for deliverance.

Don't Try to Trick God

I can genuinely advise my readers to seek God wholeheartedly. He is indeed a rewarder to those who diligently seek him. God is constantly speaking to us through different sources. We must keep our minds open at all times to be receptive to His voice. We need to talk to God on a daily basis. I cannot imagine how lost I would be if I decided to go a day without interacting with the Him—I would be so lost. My soul is renewed on a daily basis. One must never be reluctant to pray. Praying is essential for bonding with the Holy Spirit.

As I said previously, I am not a pastor—I have no position in the church—but the Holy Spirit has taught me a lot. My life has significantly changed in the past two years. God gave me wisdom and understanding and I will be forever grateful to Him. Never judge a book by its cover—and never look down at a neighbor that seems to be struggling with issues. No one knows the plan God has for his life. God is famous for using the outcasts of the world and making them into somebody of worth. I have no life without Him.

Living in constant sin is taking a big risk. I cannot say when you die you will go to hell because no man knows the heart of another but God. But there is such peace that comes with living life the right way. What does it really profit a man to gain the whole world and lose his soul? Please don't try to trick God.

One thing that my friends can attest about me is that I would never ever cover up my sins—even as a Christian. When I mess up, I always confess it openly. I confess to my friends and other sisters in Christ. There were times when even my Christian sisters would be mad at me for throwing my business out in the street like that, but I could never have concealed something of that magnitude or even something of a lesser magnitude.

My entire life is an open book. I am not asking you guys to throw your business out in the street like that, but there must be someone you can trust. I was fortunate in the fact that God had blessed me with numerous people I could share my darkest secrets with. I remember walking to my church and having to reveal my secrets to my pastor. I needed that healing; it was not until that period of honestly coming clean that God was able to fully work into my life.

Our aim is to please God—not man. If we cannot openly confess our sins, then we cannot please God the way in which we ought to. Who cares that I had a couple more guys than some other women? Who cares that I experimented with almost every possible sexual act? I am not the same person I was. Jesus saved me and He can do the same for you. Guys, I want to share this prayer with you. I think it was the powerful prayer that Jesus said before He was crucified. I changed it around a little bit.

> Hear me, Father. Rise up and defend me. Save me from the traps they set for me. Shelter me, oh Lord, I trust in you. In you I take refuge. Father, you can do all things. Please, Father, give me the strength to fight and defeat the Spirit of sexual immorality in Jesus' mighty name.

I don't think that I would have been able to accomplish anything in life without God. There were moments in my life where I was so lonely and I just wanted to die. I messed around with men because I did not think I had any other purpose. Ladies, please don't underestimate yourselves. I don't care what challenges you are up against now. Nothing is impossible for God.

Can I share a little secret with you? I believe with my whole heart that God has a special place in his heart for people that are broken. The way God took care of me when I was walking in sin—wow—only a sincere Being can do that.

My heart also goes out to a lot of people who are involved in occult practices. Please don't engage in that. It is evil. I saw the way my mother's life was affected by association with that false religion.

Conclusion

For those of you who knew me before I became a Christian, it is obvious that I am no longer the type of person I once was. Jesus has saved me. He really has transformed my mind and soul. Each day, I strive to be more like Him. My past cannot define who I am. I refuse to let disappointments, broken relationships, and financial difficulties deter me from the things of God.

I have been through lots of disappointment and was living a life contrary to the will of God, but He was merciful and gracious enough to give me another chance at life. I am no longer living a life characterized by sin. I am honest and I try to live a transparent life. It really does not matter what sins you have committed in the past—God is always waiting to forgive.

Sometimes, situations make us stronger. My Father has taught me how to be content in any situation. I hope that this book will touch the lives of many broken people all over the world—especially those who have lost hope. You have a friend in Jesus. He doesn't care what you are going through—no problem is too big for Him to handle. Just cry out to Him, and He will see you through. My life is a perfect example—God has delivered me from a lot of things and He has given me a reason to smile again.

I sometimes ask myself where my life would be without Jesus. I am confident in who I am today. I am very grateful for the people that God has brought into my life to encourage me along the way. I know that—as long as there is a God—I am bound to make it. I am bound to reach my destiny. I am not going to allow anything or anyone to cause me to compromise who I am in Christ. I cannot end this book without writing a letter to God to thank Him for everything. After all, He is the reason why you are reading this book.

> My sweet and adorable heavenly Father, thank you for all the good things you have done in my life. Father, can you believe it, the book You promised me is finally here? I have people reading my message. I still cannot believe it is real. You really came through for me big time. I could not have done it without You in my life. Father, please forgive me for all of my sins and help me to surrender to you 100 percent without any doubts. Father, You are awesome. Do You remember when You told me that You were among those who would help me?

Well, it is the truth. Thank You for loving me and teaching me how to love. Lots of love and kisses.

Your beautiful daughter, lover, and friend,
Hermie
In JESUS' name

My Imaginative Response from God

My beautiful Hermie, I am so happy to hear you express your love for me in such a profound manner. It really means a lot to have you in my life. I am happy with most of the choices you have made, and I am certain that, as you grow to love me more, you will reflect more and more of me each day. I want you to know that you will always be special in my heart. You will always be the girl that brings a smile to my heart and is not afraid to share her deepest secrets with me. I admire your openness and honesty in writing this book. It will be a bestseller, and it will reach millions of women over the world, but please remember that wherever life carries you, never turn back on the promises we made to each other. I will be there guiding you and protecting you with my eyes. You can always count on my support. I enjoy your kisses; they are pure and genuine as I am pure and genuine. Don't let people's opinions of you prevent you from reaching the stars. Please, Hermie, don't forget what I taught you: love your enemies, love those who Spitefully want to use you. I love you, my princess. Please, Hermie, remember always, I did it for love.

Lots of love and kisses,
Your heavenly Father/lover/best friend

Please let this be a tool to help you and also keep me in your prayers. I really appreciate you taking the time from your busy schedule to read this book. I am convinced that sin will no longer have dominion over your lives. I love you very much.

Walking in Victory

I conclude with this prayer.

> Heavenly Father, may everyone who reads this book experience the true power of Your love. Touch their lives in the same manner in which You have touched mine. Deliver their souls from the pits of hell and restore a right spirit in them. Give them the strength to fight against the enemy and bless their lives and the lives of everyone they come in contact with. In Jesus' mighty name. Amen.

CPSIA information can be obtained at www.ICGtesting.com
Printed in the USA
LVOW091420161011

250589LV00002B/17/P